Waterman Thomas Hewett

The Frisian Language and Literature

A historical study

Waterman Thomas Hewett

The Frisian Language and Literature
A historical study

ISBN/EAN: 9783337085193

Printed in Europe, USA, Canada, Australia, Japan

Cover: Foto ©Paul-Georg Meister /pixelio.de

More available books at **www.hansebooks.com**

THE

FRISIAN LANGUAGE

AND

LITERATURE

A HISTORICAL STUDY

BY

W T HEWETT

ITHACA, N. Y.

FINCH & APGAR.

1879.

THE FRISIAN
LANGUAGE AND LITERATURE:.

A HISTORICAL STUDY.

I. EARLY EXTENT OF FRISIA.

1. ·CLASSICAL REFERENCES TO FRISIA.

Pliny, who wrote about 17 A. D., says: "In the Rhine itself is
the most renowned island of the Batavi and the Cannenefates and
other islands of the Frisians, Chauci, Frisiavones, Sturii and Mar-
sacii, which are scattered between Helinium and Flevum. These
are the names of the two mouths into which the Rhine divides. It
empties its waters to the north into the lakes there, and to the west
into the Maas."[1] The two branches of the Rhine here mentioned
are the eastern and western. The eastern was formed from the
Sala or Yssel with which the waters of the Rhine were connected
by the canal of Drusus, and which flowed through Lake Flevo and
entered the sea between the islands of Terschelling and Ameland.
Its lower course bore later the name of the Fli.[2] The western

---

[1] In Rheno autem ipso nobilissima Batavorum insula et Cannenefatium
et aliae Frisiorum, Chaucorum, Frisiavonum, Sturiorum, Marsaciorum
quae sternunter inter Helinium et Flevum : ita appellantur ostia in quae
effusus Rhenus a septentrione in lacus ab occidente in amnem Mosam se
spargit.—*Pliny, Nat. Hist.*, Lib. IV, c. 29.

[2] See *Alting, Notitia Germaniæ Inferioris Antiquæ*, p. 82. He holds
that Helvloet and Briel (Bree-Hel) are remains of the name Helinium.
See also *Stratingh, Aloude Staat des Vaderlands*, vol I, p. 144. The
central branch of the Rhine called the Old Rhine enters the sea near
Leiden.

branch was the Vahalis (Waal) which entered the sea near the present Rotterdam.

It is noticeable that the Chauci are here associated with the Frisians, as they are later their neighbors to the east on the coasts of the North Sea.

Tacitus, writing about 100 A. D., describes the Frisians as dwelling along the Rhine and among great lakes as far as the ocean. They were divided into Greater and Lesser Frisians, according to the resources of the two nations." [1]

The Lesser Frisians, or Frisiabones, are supposed to have resided between the mouths of the Maas and the Fli, in South and North Holland.[2] An apparent branch of the Frisians bearing the name Frisiabones resided in the district of Limburg on the borders of Liege and South Brabant.[3]

Ptolemy, who wrote between 139 and 161 A. D., places the Frisians north of the Bructeri extending along the coast as far as the river Ems. To the east between the Ems and the Weser resided the Lesser Chauci, then the Greater Chauci between the Weser and the Elbe, and next in order upon the neck of the Cimbrian peninsula the Saxons.[4] The Chauci here appear as occupying what was later East Frisia. Tacitus, however, places the Greater Chauci between the Ems and the Weser and the Lesser Chauci between the Weser and the Elbe.[5] The home of the Chauci seems to have been between the Ems and the Weser, and those residing to the east of the Weser simply an outlying colony.

---

[1] Angrivarios et Chamavos a tergo Dulgubinii et Chasuarii cludunt, aliaeque gentes haud perinde memoratae a fronte Frisii excipiunt, maioribus minoribusque Frisiis vocabulum est ex modo virium   Utraeque nationes usque ad Oceanum Rheno praetexuntur ambiuntque immensos insuper lacus et Romanis classibus navigatos.—*Germ.*, c. 34.

[2] See *Alting*, I, 71, and *Stratingh*, II, p. 111.

[3] *Pliny*, Lib. IV, c. 31.

[4] Τὴν δὲ παρωκεανῖτιν κατέχουσιν ὑπὲρ μὲν τοὺς Βουσακτέρους οἱ Φρίσιοι μέχρι τοῦ Ἀμισίου ποταμοῦ; μέτα δὲ τούτους Καῦχοι οἱ μικροὶ μέχρι τοῦ Οὐισουργίου ποταμοῦ εἶτα Καῦχοι οἱ μείζους μέχρι τοῦ Ἄλβιος ποταμοῦ; ἐφεξῆς δὲ ἐπὶ τὸν αὐχένα τῆς κιμβρικῆς χερσονήσου Σάξονες.—*Geog.*, Lib. II, c. XI.

[5] Sunt vero et in septentrione visae nobis Chaucorum qui maiores minoresque appellantur.—*Pliny*, XVI, c. I.   The description of their country which follows applies strikingly to East Frisia and the district of Saterland.

Strabo, who wrote earlier at the beginning of the Christian era,
does not mention the Frisians. In a list of nations dwelling between the Rhine and the ocean he mentions the Sicambri, Chamavi,
Bructeri, Cimbri, Chauci, Chaulki, Ampsiani and many others.[1] In
another list embracing these tribes he omits similarly the Chauci.
The term 'Αμψιανοί is a geographical one, denoting the dwell-
ers along the Ems and may well have included the Frisians. In a
Notitia Gentium[2] written at the beginning of the fourth century,
the Frisians are placed between the Chamavi, the inhabitants of
Hamaland and the Amsivarii. A similar list of the fourth century,[3]
ascribed in some codices to Julius Caesar places the Frusiones or
Frisiones, as appears in another manuscript, next to the Cannifates
who occupied the western part of the Batavian island. The Geog-
rapher of Ravenna, who wrote in the last half of the seventh century, places Dorostate (Duurstede) on the north bank of the Rhine
in the country of the Frisians "in Frigonum or Frixonum patria."
The Frisians, according to him, extended still farther to the south
into the district of Testerbant adjoining Flanders.

At one time the Frisians advanced up the Rhine and established
themselves temporarily on the lands reserved for the military colo-
nists between Wesel and Düsseldorf, but were soon obliged to retire
across the Rhine.[4] The first Roman to come in contact with the
Frisians was Drusus, who, after the construction of his famous canal,
connecting the Rhine and the Sala or Yssel, sailed into Lake Flevo,
and received the submission of the Frisian nation. The campaign
of Germanicus against the Saxons was through Frisia to the Ems.
Later the Romans suffered a terrible defeat in the Baduhenna forest
by the Frisians,[5] but were afterwards subdued under the vigorous
military administration of Corbulo, and became regular allies of
Rome. The Roman governor placed them under the government of

[1] Πρὸς δὲ τῷ ὠκεανῷ Σούγαμβροί τε καὶ Χάμαβοι καὶ
Βρούκτεροι καὶ Κίμβροι Καῦκοί τε καὶ Καούλκοι καὶ 'Αμψιανοί καὶ ἄλλοι πλείους.—Geog., Lib. VII, c. I.

[2] Amsivari, Angri, Chattuarii, Chamavi, Frisiavi, Amsivarii.—Müllen-
hoff, Germania Antiqua, p. 157.

[3] Quae gentes sint in provinciis oceani orientis, Catti, Cauci, Cerisci,
Usippi, Quadi, Frusiones, Cannifates, Theutoni, Cimbri.—Ibid, p. 159.

[4] Annal., XIII, 54, A. D. 59.

[5] Annal., IV, c. 72, 73.

a senate, magistrates and laws.[1] Only scattered traces bear witness to the relations of the Frisians to Rome during the next few centuries. Frisian soldiers served in the Roman armies in England, and in Italy where they were members of the Emperor's body guard.[2]

THE RELATIONS OF THE FRISIANS TO THE OTHER GERMAN TRIBES.

The passages already quoted from classic authors show the intimate relations which existed between the Chauci and the Frisians. The former are associated with them, according to Tacitus, in the district between the two arms of the Rhine. They are also placed as their neighbors on the east, in the region between the Ems and the Weser. The references in Beowulf. to Frisia are of interest. The sixteenth, seventeenth, thirty-fifth and fortieth cantos relate to a war between the Frisians and the Danes. The Traveler's Tale relates[3] how Fin, son of Folcwalda, king of the Frisians, fights with Hnaef a Hocing, the leader of the Scildings in Finnesburh or Finneshâm and slays him. Hengest the Dane assumes command, a truce is negotiated and hostages are given. Both armies go together to Friesland. In the winter the strangers are prevented by frightful storms and ice from returning home. They think more of vengeance and the slaughter of their kindred than of seeking their native land. At last reinforced they attack again the Frisians and slay their king, and carry captive Hildeburh, the daughter of Hôce to Denmark. Hygilâc, King of the Goths, falls[4] in a battle with the Frisians. Beowulf escapes by swimming to his own country.

The name Chauci appears in Hugas (Hockings) who inhabit Frisia, and perhaps in that of Hôce, the father of Hildeburh. That Fin the Frisian king ruled over the Jutes as well as the Frisians is inadmissible. No reference is made to the Jutes in this song.[5] There

---

[1] *Annal.*, XIII, 54, A. D. 59.

[2] In 1836 there was found at Watemore, near Cirencester, a memorial stone of a Frisian Knight, who was a member of the Thracian cohort serving in England. Other Roman remains found at the same place belong to the time of Diocletian and Constantine, and this inscription is probably to be assigned to the same period. For inscriptions found in Italy, see in *Gruter*, Nos. 12 and 13; also *Orelli*. See also *Dr. Leemans, in the Vreie Fries*, vol. III, p. 5.

[3] *Boewulf*, XVI, 1052-1129.

[4] Lines 1202, 1511, 2356-2359.

[5] The word Eotenas has been shown by Rieger to apply to both Frisians and Danes.—*Zeitschrift für deutsche Philologie*, vol. III, p. 400.

is no distinction in the terms employed in the poem between North and West Frisia, as is often claimed.[1] Whenever the term is used it seems to apply to the Frisia of the main land, not to the North Frisia of the peninsula. Freswäle may denote a frontier castle. Grimm[2] calls attention to the similar mode in which the Frisians, Chauci and Bructeri are characterized. These three tribes of northeastern Germany are each divided into Lesser and Greater, a distinction which was employed among no other German tribes, even though many were much larger and occupied a greater extent of country than these. Grimm would also make the Bructeri closely related to the Chauci and Frisians, though their political action was often different.[3] He claims that the mighty race of the Chauci, whom Tacitus called the noblest of all the Germans, could not be extinguished, but that being so closely related to the Frisians they were absorbed in them. The east and north Frisians are the descendants of the Chauci, while the west Frisians have retained their name and original seat.[4]

Eichhorn holds conclusively that the Frisian name includes the tribes of the Chauci. The Saxons must be regarded as later immigrants into East Frisia, the original abode of the Chauci.[5]

Grimm calls attention to the fact that in the remains of the epic poetry of northeastern Germany, the Frisians and Chauci constantly appear, while the Germans of the interior, of Saxony and of Swabia, take no part.[6] In Gudrun, whose composition is of a later date, but

---

[1] By Heyne, Beowulf, p. 109. The terms used for Frisia are in line 1127 Frysland, in 2916 Fresnaland, while in 2358, it is the plural Freslondum.

[2] *Geschichte der deutschen Sprache*, 676.

[3] See *Tacitus, Annals*, I, 60.

[4] Nach allem diesem stellen sich Friesen und Chauken nur als verwandte Zweige desselben Volkschlags dar, als der südwestliche und nordöstliche, und man begreift warum der Chaukische Name allmählich ganz erlosch. Ostfriesen und Nordfriesen scheinen mir Nachkömmlinge der alten Chauken, Westfriesen die der eigentlichen Friesen. Wohnten die alten Chauken an der Seeküste, so müssen sie nothwendig die Striche inne gehabt haben, auf welche nachher auch der friesische Name erstreckt wurde. Vernichtet worden sein kann der mächtige Chaukische Stamm nicht; er wechselte bloss die Benennung.—*Ges. der deut. Spr.*, p. 471.

[5] Der Friesische Name begreift daher unzweifelhaft die Chaukischen Völker da die Sachsen in deren Gegenden nur als Einwanderer betrachtet werden können.—*Eichhorn, Deut. Staats-und Rechtsgeschichte*, vol. I, p. 50 and note to p. 51.

[6] *Ges. der deut. Spr.*, 471.

is based upon early legends and historical events associated with which that region, we have the proper names as centres of incident. Holzâne laut (Holstein) 1374, 3. Matelâne, 760, 3 (Matlinge (?) in South Holland), Selânt (Zeeland), Sêwen (also Zeeland, possibly named from the Suevi), 706, 1. Tenelant (Denmark), Westerwalt (possibly Westerwold) 945. Dietmers 639, (Dietmarsch) as well as Frieslant.

Hetele, king of the Hegelinge, is the ruler of Friesland, of Ditmarsch and Wûleis (the district of the Waal).

> " Er was ze Friesen herre, wazzer unde lant ;
> Dietmers unde Wâleis was in sîner haut."—208, 1.

Môrunc is lord of the march of Waleis.

> " Môrunc der snelle dâ her von Friesen reit."—271.

Irolt, a vassal of Hetele, is the ruler of Ortland (Northland), and a part of Frisia.

> " Ouch kumt uns her Irolt, des mag ich wohl jehen,
> Er bringet vil der Frisen, als ich mich kan versehen,
> Und ouch der Holsaèzen ; daz sint ziere helde."—1374.

> " Irolt von Ortrîche und Môrunc von Friesenlant."—480.

2. EXTENT OF FRISIA DURING THE FRANKISH PERIOD.

The greatest extent of the Frisian race and name seems to have been attained in the sixth and seventh centuries. The great movement of the German tribes in the fifth and sixth centuries erased all traces of Roman dominion. The tribal dominions and relations were re-adjusted in the period following. The Frisians extended on the east to the Weser and the Elbe, and occupied the islands along the coast of Schleswig. Southward they occupied both banks of the Rhine, Utrecht, Gelderland, Antwerp and Bruges. Between 600 and 785 A. D., the conflict between the Franks and the Frisians, occurred. Dagobert captured Utrecht then occupied by the Frisians, and called Wiltenburg, and founded in 630 A. D. the first Christian church in the North Netherlands. The period which followed is that of the labors of the first Anglo-Saxon missionaries among the Frisians. Possibly earlier under the Roman dominion missionaries began labor in the Netherlands, but no traces of such efforts were left. Only as the power of the Frankish kings was felt by the Frisians, could missionary operations among them be safely carried on. Pepin of Heristal resolved in 689 or 692 to bring the Frisians under the Frankish yoke. He defeated them and made them pay tribute and receive Christian missionaries. Radbod, their king, the brave defender of the liberties of his country, rose again but was defeated at Dorestadt, now Wijk-bij-Duurstede, and Utrecht came again under Pepin's dominion. Radbod's daughter, Theudesnede, was given in marriage to Grimoald, Pepin's son, A. D. 697. The Frisians fought again a great battle under Radbod, at Cologne, in 716, and defeated the East Franks. Charles Martel re-assembled his army and won a victory over the Frisians at Stablo. He followed them into Frisia, and defeated them in a battle on the Middle Sea. The Frisians then sued for peace. Radbod, their king, died in 719 A.D. Adegild II succeeded him, but the Franks no longer permitted him the title of king, but that of hertog or duke. The Frisians now followed the Franks in their wars. Later they joined the league against the Franks, formed by the Saxon duke Wittekind which embraced the Danes under their king Siegfried, and the Frisians under their duke Radbod. This formidable alliance was finally overcome by Charlemagne, and the independence of Frisia forever lost, A. D. 785. Later the country was governed by Frankish counts, deputies and stadholders.[1] It becomes necessary to define the exact boundaries of Frisia as an aid in determining the extent of the Frisian language, as it is probable that the Lex Frisionum received its present form substantially at this time.

Frisia was divided into three parts, and these divisions are mentioned in the divisions of the Empire of 846 and 870. In the division of the Empire in 839, Lothair received the duchy of Frisia which at that time extended to the Maas.[2] In the division of 870, Lewis the German received East and Central Frisia.[3]

---

[1] *Foeke Sjoerds, Hist. Jaarboeken,* vol. I, p. 406, ff.

[2] " Ducatum Frisiae usque Mosam."—*Hlud.* I, *Capit. Pertz, Mon. Ger.* vol. III, 373.

[3] Et haec ist divisio quam sibi Hludowicus accepit. De Frisia duas

Western Frisia was situated between the river Sinkfal in the vicinity of Bruges in Flanders and the Fli; Central Frisia between the Fli and the Lauwers; Eastern Frisia between the Lauwers and the Weser. These divisions gave rise to certain special provisions in the Frisian laws, and often marked the limits in which those laws prevailed. The passages in the Lex Frisionum which specify these districts are the following: "Haec lex inter Laubachi et Flchum custoditur, caeterum inter Flehum et Sincfalam pro huiusmodi causa talis est consuetudo."—Tit. XIV, 1. "Apud occidentales Fresiones inter Flehi et Sincfalam."—Additio Sapientum, Tit. III, § XLIX. "Inter Fli et Sincfalam."—Tit. I, § X. "Hoc inter Laubaci et Sincfalam."—Tit. IV, § VI. "Inter Laubachi et Wiseram et cis Fli similiter."—Tit. I, § III.

The position of Sincfal as a harbor or bay is implied in the mention of the length of the voyage from Ripa in Denmark to Sincfal, given by Adam of Bremen, as two days and two nights, while from Sincfal to Prol, the opposite point on the English coast, it is specified as two days and one night.[1]

The Tenth Kûre, composed about 1200 A. D., specifies as a grant from Charlemagne that the Frisians should not be required to serve as soldiers beyond the Weser on the east and the Fli on the west, and no further to the south than would be possible for them to return in an evening, in order to protect their country against the sea and foreign enemies.[2]

partes de regno quod Lotharius habuit. Et haec ist divisio quam Carolus de eodem regno sibi accepit, — de Frisia tertiam partem.—*Annal., Bert.*, Pars III, *Pertz*, I, 489, 490.

[1] De Ripa in Flandriam ad Cincfal velificari potest duobus diebus et totidem noctibus. De Cincfal ad Prol in Angliam duobus diebus et una nocte. Illud est ultimum caput Angliae versus austrum et est processus illuc de Ripa angulosus inter austrum et occidentem.—*Scholion, 96, M. Adami, Gesta Ham.*, Lib. IV. The author, a canon of Bremen, died about 1125.

[2] Decima petitio est: Frisiones non oportere exercitum ducere, ulterius quam ad Wiseram versus orientem, et versus occidentem usque Fli; versus austrum non remotius quam possint in vespere redire ut eorum possint patriam tenuere contra fluctus et gentilem exercitum. Petivit autem rex Karolus quod ipsi ultra proficisci vellent in orientem usque Hiddesekkere et in occidentem usque Singfallum. Et obtinuerunt id Frisiones apud Karolum quod ipsi bannos suos non ultra servarent quam in orientum ad Wiseram et in occidentem usque Fli.—*Friesische Rechtsquellen Richthofen*, pp. 17, 18.

The Rustringer text has: "Thit is thiu tiande liodkest, thet wi Frisa

Sincfal is undoubtedly Zwin, a small river in Flanders, as Maerlant, the Flemish poet, who lived from about 1220 to 1300 A. D., says:

> "Al Vrieslant verre ende na
> Tusscen der Elven end Sincval
> Rekent men te Sassenal."—I Partie Boek, I, c. 33.

> "Teenen tiden quam sulc geval
> Den volke dat tusscen Sincval
> Enter Wesere sat alleene.
> Dat daer was ene scare gemene
> Ende altemale Vriesen hieten."

> "Tusscen der Wesere en ten Zwene
> Dat tien tiden hiet Sincval."

> "Tfole dat upter zee woent al
> Tusscen der Wesere ende Sincval
> Dat wi Frieslant heten bi namen."

> "Alle die lieden ghemeelike
> Die lancs der zee saten hene
> Tusscen der Wesere an ten Zwene
> Dat tien tiden hiet Sincval
> Wart ane Gode bekeert al
> Bi Willeborde, bi Willade
> Ende bi Bonifacis predicade."
> —III Partie Boek, VIII, c. XCIII.

In the Rijm Cronijk of Melis Stoke, written between 1283–1287, we find:

> "Die Scelt was dat west end Sine,
> Also sie valt in de zee
> Oest streckende mine no mee
> Van toter Lavecen ofter Elven."—Book I, 46.

---

ne thuron nene hiriferd fara thruch thes kininges bon, ni nen bodthing firor sitta, tha Wester to tha Fli and aster to there Wisura, suther to there Wepilinge and north to heves ouere. Tha welde thi kinig Kerl tha liode firor leda wester to Sinkfalon and aster to Hiddisekre.—Tenth Kesta.

It is possible that Charlemagne made this concession, but in fact the Frisians formed a part of his army in his campaign across the Elbe, and to the south against the Dalmatians, and in Spain where, at Roncesvalles, their last king, the grandson of Radbod, was killed.—*Enhardi, Annal. Fuld.*, A. D. 789.

" Nu west in Vlandren so verre comen
Dat Brueghe stont in 's Coninx's hant,
En bider zee aldat lant
Sonder die Dam metten Swene
Also oestwaert 'tlant ghemene."— VI, 1146.

" Van hemsse haer Jan bedochte,
Dat hi selve voer ter Sluse
En bernede daer vele huese
En quam weder sonder strijt.
Doe gheviel een an der tijt
Dat de Vresen voeren over
Tote Caetsant an den hoever,
En stichten roof en brant."—IV, 914.

" En trecte opt uterst van Zeelant
Tote Vlissinghe on dat zant
En zom toten zouten lande.—IV, 907. "

In a charter of 1241, given by Thomas, count of Flanders and Hennegau, Muiden is made a city free from duties, also the district around Damme and the harbor called in the vulgar language Sincfal. The name indicates therefore a bay or harbor accessible to sea-going ships. It extended between Sluis and Damme and north of Bruges.[1] This stream called the Zwin (Sine) entered the Hunte or Wester-Scheldt which here separates Flanders (Cadsand) and the island of Walcheren. Zeeland then included a district south of the Scheldt, and within the boundaries of Frisia. The see of Utrecht then embraced Bruges. The Hunte is not mentioned before 1161. It was then an insignificant stream, and did not attain its present size until the fifteenth century.[2]

Ruoteberus, who slew his brother Baldwin, is said to have made in the year 1071 an hostile expedition into Frisia which borders on Flanders.[3]

---

[1] Thomas Flandrie et Hannonie comes; fecimus apud Mudan frankam villam et concessimus omnibus illis de Muda scabingium et legem ville Brugensis . . absolvimus universos infra dictum scabinagium de Muda manentes et omni teloneo infra villam de Dam et undique infra portum qui vulgaritur appellatur Sincfal. Quoted by *Stratingh*, I, 115. See also *Kluit. Hist. Crit. Com. Holland*, II, 1032, for a charter of 1275, containing a similar grant.

[2] *Van den Bergh, Handboek der Middel-Ned. Geog.*, p. 82.

[3] Ruoteberus atque in Fresiam, quae confinio est Flandriae irruptionem fecit.—*Lamberti, Annal., Pertz*, VII, 181.

Walcheron appears first as an island in 837 A. D.[1] Frisian institutions still exist in Zeeland, as the divisions of estates according to the number of cattle. Frisian words and forms are still found in Dutch Flanders. Vlaardingen near Rotterdam also bears the name constantly of a Frisian city.[2]

The eastern limit of West Frisia is called in the Frisian laws Fli, Flehi or Flehum, and is of frequent mention in the monastic chronicles and charters.[3] The early Roman writers say that the eastern branch of the Rhine emptied into the lake Flevo,[4] flowed through it and sought the sea at Flevum, between the present islands of Vlieland and Terschelling. The islands of Texel and Vlieland were at that time united. The river flowed past Stavoren and along the present coast of Friesland. Hence the present provinces of North and South Holland, as well as the islands of Zeeland, formed a part of West Frisia. The name Holland, Holtland or forest-land, appears in the early records of the see of Utrecht. The name was first applied to the district around Dordrecht, along the Maas and the Meriwede. The separation from Central Frisia, both by rivers and the lake of Flevo, produced early differences in the laws of the two sections and political separation. Holland became the property of the Counts of Holland. They bore the title Counts of Frisia until 1083, when

---

[1] Nordmanni tributum exactantes in Walchram venerunt.—*Annal., Fuld. Pertz*, I, 361. Ea tempestate Nordmanni irruptione solita Frisiam irruentes in insula quae Walcria dicitur imperatos aggressi . . et ad Dorestadum eadem Frisia pervenerunt.—*Annal., Bert.* A. D. 837. Compare. Igitur imperator disposita Frisiae maritimaeque custodia; that is, Zeeland and Frisia ; similarly Campania et maritima is used in classical Latin where but one district is meant.—*Annal. Bert., Pertz*, I, 430, A.D. 837.

[2] Vlaardingen sic enim haec regio Frisionum vocatur.—*Alpert De Divers, Temp. Pertz*, VI, 719, A. D. 1018. Deinde exercitum navalem per Renum duxit in Fresiam contra Gotefridum eius que adiutorem Diodericum, ibique duas urbes munitissimas cepit, Rinesburg et Flaerdingen.—*Lamb. Annal.*, A. D. 1047, *Pertz*, VII, 154.

[3] Apud occidentales Frisiones inter Flehi et Sincfalam.—*Lex Fris. Ad.*, III, 58, XLIX. "Ecclesiam in occidentali Fresia in Villa Medenblec."—*Pertz*, II, 389, A. D. 1118. Fresones occidentales qui habitant trans vadum Occenvorth in agros oppiduli Alcmare conscenderunt.—*Pertz*, XVI, A. D. 1166.

[4] Later called Aelmere. "Trans stagnum quod in lingua eorum dicitur Aelmere."—*Vita S. Bonifat, Pertz*, vol. II, 34. The present name Zuider Zee does noes not appear until the thirteenth century.

Dirk V styled himself "Theodore, by the grace of God Count of Holland."[1]

The city of Egmont was long the boundary between the country of Holland and Frisia. The Fli as a division line was early recognized. Wittekind is said to have destroyed the churches and expelled the priests, and forced the people as far as the Fli, to return to paganism.[2] The Western Frisians do not seem to have joined in the league against Charlemagne, composed of East Frisians, Danes and Saxons.

The western boundary of Central Frisia was the Laubachi or Lauwers, at present a small stream flowing north into the Lauwers-Zee, and forming the boundary between the provinces of Friesland and Groningen. It seems early to have been a division line and the Frisians who resided beyond it adhered longer to their old paganism. Charlemagne constituted Liudeger a teacher in · the five districts which lay to the east of the Lauwers, (Labeke).[3] Similarly Gregory, the successor of Boniface as bishop of Utrecht, preached to the east of the Lauwers.[4] There are also in charters constant references to the Lauwers as forming a boundary line between Central and East Frisia, as "all the lands from Stavoren as far as the

---

[1] Quot autem in Hollandia vel Frisia.—*Annal.*, *Erphard*, A. D. 124-9. *Pertz*, XVI, 37. Wilhelmus Romanorum rex occiditur a Fresonibus Medemblik prope Hollandiam morantibus.—*Annal.*, *Stad.* A. D. 1276. Comitatus Hollandensis et Fresonicus et unum pertinent comitem et utriusque populi confinium est quasi divisio est villa Ekmundensis.—*Pertz*, XVI, 466. Fresones extremi versus occidentem qui dicuntur Westlingi (West Flingi).—*Mat. Annal.*, II, 157, quoted by Richthofen XV. "Theodericus dei gratia Hollandensis comes."—*Kluit.* II, 138, quoted by Van den Bergh, p. 219.

[2] Radix sceleris Widukint evertit Fresones a via Dei combussitque ecclesias et expulit Dei famulos et usque ad Fleo fluvium fecit Fresones fidem relinquere et immolare idolis juxta morem erronis pristini.— *Vita S. Liud.*, A. D. 782.

[3] Gloriosus princeps Karolus constituit eum (Liudgerum) doctorem in gente Fresonum ab orientali parti fluminis Labeki super pagos quinque Hugmerchi, Hunusga, Fivilga, Emsiga, Federitga.—*Pertz*, IV, 410, A. D. 785.

[4] Doctrina sua beatus Gregorius Traiectum, antiquam civitatem, et vicum famosum Dorstad cum illa inradiavit parte Fresoniae, quae tunc temporus Christianitatis censebatur; idem usque in ripam occidentalem fluminis quod dicitur Lagbeki, ubi confinium erat Christianorum Fresonum ac paganorum cunctis diebus Pippini regis.—*Vita S. Greg. Acta SS. Benedic. Saec.* III, P. II, p. 295.

Borne and the rest of Frisia from the Borne to the Lauwers,"[1] the "lands of Frisia situated between the Ems and the Lauwers."[2] The eastern boundary of Frisia at the promulgation of the Lex Frisionum was the Weser river. Certain portions of the laws apply to the country between the Lauwers and the Weser:[3] "all the lands, islands and districts in all Frisia between the Weser and Meeresdiep," "all Frisia from the Zuider-Zee to the Weser."[4] We thus find Frisia at the time in which the Lex Frisionum was in force divided into three parts; West Frisia, which included a strip of country in Flanders along the southern shore of West Scheldt, Zeeland[5] and Holland. Central Frisia between the Fli, the eastern shore of the Zuider-Zee and the Lauwers, separating the provinces of Friesland and Groningen. This has been the permanent seat of the Frisians where the Lex Frisionum originated, and where the language is still retained in use. That these divisions of Frisia had a certain centre of union and a government by a law with in the main similar provisions is shown by the quotations already given.

3. THE EXTENT OF FRISIA TO THE NORTH.

The extent of the Frisian dominion to the north, and the period in which the North Frisian islands were occupied, cannot be determined with accuracy. Ptolemy speaks of a tribe of $\Phi\iota\rho\alpha\tilde{\iota}\delta\sigma\iota$ as dwelling in Skandia, or southern Sweden. There is a district also in West Gothland having the name Frisjö. This may indicate an

---

[1] Omnes a Stavria usque ad Bornedam reliqua vero pars Fresiae a Borneda usque ad Lavicam, A. D. 1230. Quoted by *Richthofen, Lex Frisionum*, p. XIII.
[2] Allen sinen landen, luden, onderzaten ende hulperen gezeten tusschen der Lauwers ende der Wezere.—*Charterboek von Friesland*, I, 389.
[3] Inter Laubachi et Wiseram et cis Fli, see in the Lex Frisionum.— *Tit.* I, 3, 4, 5, 10; IX, 13; XI; XXII.
[4] Alle de lande, eylande, en omlande omtrent 't gemeine Frieslant gelegen tuschen de Weser en 't Meersdiep.—*Brenneisen*, I, P. 2, p. 33, quoted by *Richthofen*, XIV. Des gemenen Frieslandes von der Zuderzee to der Wezere.—*Kengers Werken*, I, 125.
[5] This district from the Zwin to the Maas received in the eleventh century the name Se-land or Zeeland. The territory between the Maas and Alkmaar received the name Holtland (Holland). A small district to the north of Alkmaar still bears the name West Friesland. The German application of the term to the present province of Friesland is wrong historically, and contrary to national use.

early settlement in Scandinavia.[1] There is in Beowulf, in the battle of Finnesburg, a possible reference to an outlying border castle. In the Egilsaga of 1220 A. D. there is a refenence to the land lying between Frisia and Denmark.[2] Helgoland was in the eighth century Frisian and apparently the centre of the worship of Fosite,[3] and possibly the residence of the king Radbod.[4] The Strand Frisians are mentioned as early as the thirteenth century under that name.[5]

The inhabitants of Ditmarsch between the Elbe and the Eider were closely and early connected with the Frisians, probably both by language as well as blood. The Frisians often appear associated with them. We read that in the year 1226, many Frisians entered Ditmarsch to aid in the defense of the country against the Danes.[6]

Eichhorn holds that the Strand Frisians who resided on the west coast of Schleswig, and on the former island of Nordstrand took possession of that district after the third century.[7] Falck declares for the time of Charlemagne or somewhat earlier.[8] The occupation of this district, north of the Elbe and bordering on the Danes by a mixed population of Saxons and Franks, is manifest as early as the year 882 and shown by a letter from the Emperor Lothair to the pope, in which he says that on the borders of the empire there is a

---

[1] Corresponding to Dahlmann's view of the early residence of Frisians in the north.—*Geschichte von Dänemark*, I, 16.

[2] þeir koma til landamaeris þar er moetiz Danmörk ok Frîsland, ok lâgu þâ vit land.—Quoted by *Grimm.*, *Ges. der deut. Spr.*, p. 466.

[3] An effort has been made to connect the word *Frisian* with the Norse Fro and Freir, and the name of the Frisian goddess *Fosite*, Norse, Forseti. —*Zur Stammes-und Sagengeschichte der Friesen und Chauken, Volckmar.*

[4] Unde accepit nomen ut Heiligland dicatur.—*Vita S. Willebrord.* Fositesland appellari discimus quae sita est in confinio Danorum et Fresonum ; Sunt et aliae insulae contra Fresiam et Daniam sed nulla eorum tam memorabilis.—*M. Adami Gesta, Ham. Book*, I, 279.

[5] Rex Danorum Abel Strantfrisones ab insolentia eorum volens compescere, inopinata morte eiis est occisus.—*Pertz*, XIV, 373.

[6] Multi Frisones corruerunt in Thidemaerskia et tamen Thidemaerskia Danis subjugata est.—*Annal.*, *Ryenses, Pertz*, XVI, 407.

[7] Ich bin geneigt anzunehmen dass die Nord oder Strand Frisones des Herzogthums Schleswig seit dem dritten Jahrhundert eingewandert sind.—*Deut. Staats-und Rechtsgeschichte*, vol. I, p. 50.

[8] *Handbuch des Schleswig-Holst. Privatrechts*, I, 80.

race of Saxons and Frisians which had formerly received the Christian faith.[1]

Frisia probably extended to the south as far as the branch of the Rhine called the Waal. Utrecht[2] (Utra-jectum) which bore the name Wiltenburg was a Frisian city. It was captured by Dagobert, who founded here the first Christian chapel in the North Netherlands. The districts of Drenthe, Over-Yssel, and Utrecht were largely Frisian, though later occupied by a mixed population of Salian Franks. It is said that the Frisians, who are called Destarbenzon,[3] either because they occupied the territory of the latter or because they were closely related, won a great victory over the Normans in the year 885. The country of Teisterbaut or Testerbant, which lay between the Rhine and the Old Maas, and the countries of Betuwe and Hattuarias, occupying a part of the Batavian island, bore this name at the division of the empire in 870.[4] Deventer was originally Frisian, the name itself being Frisian.[5]

Frisian colonies were also scattered along the Rhine far to the south. Birthen between Xanten and Rheinberg, near Weser, was Frisian.[6] Mainz[7] had a large proportion of Frisian citizens, and in

---

[1] Est eniam gens in partibus nostri regni Saxonum scilicet et Frisonum commixta in confinibus Nordmannorum et Obodritorum sita quae evangelicam doctrinam iam dudum audierat et acceperat sed propter vicinitatem paganorum ex parte in firma religione constat et ex parte iam pene defecta.—*Translatio S. Alex*, A. D. 863, *Pertz*, II, 677.

A septentrione vero Nordmannos gentes ferocissimas, Ab ortu autem solis Obodritos et ab occasu Frisos a quibus sine intermissione vel foedere vel concertatione necessario finium suorum spacia tuebantur.—*Ibid.*, II, 675.

[2] Et apud Traiectum quod Fresiam respicit.—*Vita Poppon*, A. D. 1050, *Pertz*, XIII, 305. Anno dominicae incarnationis 1039, imperator Chuonradus ipso anno diem sanctam pentecostes apud Traiectum civitatem Fresiae celabravit.—*Vita Chuonrad, Imp. Pertz*, XIII, 274.

[3] Interea Frisones qui vocantur Destarbenzon.—*Annal. Fuld.* A. D. 885, *Pertz*, I, 402.

[4] Bant here denotes district, and the name of the people is a geographical one. The form Twente, in early documents Tuvanti, is the classical Tuibantes: in like manner also Drenthe must have had the form Thrianti which recalls the Tribantes of Tacitus. See *Grimm, Ges. der deut. Spr.*, 412, also *Stratingh*, Part II, 130.

Nordmanni portum qui Frisica lingua Taventeri nominatur, succend-.unt.—*Annal., Fuld. Pertz*, V, 397.

[6] Nordmanni Biorzuna ubi pars maxima Frisionum habitabat incendia concremarunt.—*Annal., Fuld.* A. D. 937.

[7] Optima pars Mogontiae civitatis ubi Frisones habitant conflagravit incendio.—*Annal., Fuld.* A. D. 886.

a description of the country around Worms by the bishop Thendola-chus A. D. 873, we find a Frisian Speier mentioned.[1] On the river Silz in this vicinity lies Friesenheim, which may have been a Fri-sian colony. We cannot suppose that the Lex Frisionum ever pre-vailed to the south of the Rhine. The Salian law was early intro-duced along the Yssel. Bequests were made, not according to Frisian law, but according to Ripuarian and Salian law.[2] Wijk-bij-Duurstede is frequently mentioned as Frisian.[3] Meppel was Saxon, as early as the eighth century.[4]

It has been attempted to determine the limits of Frisian territory by the appearance of the termination *um* in proper names of places. This has been held to be a characteristic of Frisian occupation everywhere. This *um* is in many cases a relic of the older *hem*, Frankish *heim*, Saxon *em*, English *ham* as in Durham. In a regis-ter of the Abbey of Werden of the year 983, we find Falconhem (Valkum), Sahsinghem (Saaksum), Werfhem (Warfum), Midlist-hem (Middelstum). The termination *heim* or *hem* appears but a few times in names of places in the Netherlands. In Helgoland alone in 800 A. D., there were forty places having the termination *um*. In 1200 A. D., the names of eighty-two places in North Frisia ended in *um*, while in West Frisia there were seventy-two places having that termination: in East Frisia twenty-four, in Nordstrand nineteen, in Eiderstedt four. Over seventy-six places in the present province of Frisia end in *um*. The termination *um* ap-pears in the names of but few places outside of the provinces of Friesland, Groningen and the west coast of Schleswig-Holstein. This termination predominates in names of places on the islands of

---

[1] De loco qui dicitur Frisonen-Spira usque ad Rhenum ipsi Frisones restauranda muralia procurent. Rudolsheim, Gunsheim, Turkheim, Alsheim, Mettenheim a super dicta Spira usque ad locum qui Rheni-Spira vocatur provideant.—*Annal.*, *Worm*, A. D. 873. These places lie north of Worms, between Worms and Oppenheim.

[2] In a grant given in 855, we find, "Ego Folkerus, quasdam proprie-tatis meae res in pago Hamuland in comitatu Wigmanni, nec non in Batuwe, coram testibus secundum legem Ripuariam et Salicam, nec non secundum *ewa* Fresonum tradidi."—*Lecomblet, Rheinisches Urkundenbuch*, I, 30. Richthofen claims that the specification of "not according to the law of the Frisians," is an interpolation from another diploma.

[3] Inde egressi per Dorstatum et vicinia Fresonum transeuntes.—*Vita S. Anskarii*, c. 8.

[4] Oppidum est in Saxonia notum plurimis Meppea nominatum.—*Vita S. Liud.*, Lib. II, 25. *Acta Benedict Saec.*, IV.

Föhr and on the southern half of the island of Sylt. To the east
the names of places are Danish and Low German, with few Frisian
forms. The termination *büll*, Dan. *bôl* and *bölle*, possibly *büttel* in
Wolfenbüttel, meaning a cottage, which does not appear on old
charts of West and East Frisia, is found in the earliest records of
North Frisia. On the west coast of Schleswig-Holstein and on the
North Frisian islands, more than a hundred names of places have
this ending.

II. LITERATURE.

That the Frisians had early a distinct form of speech is evident
from the early mention of their language, even before we possess
literary remains. We find the *Frisica lingua* mentioned in the annals of Fulda of 882 A. D., also in the life of St. Boniface, *Fresonum
lingua*.[1] This language always bears the name Frisian, and does not
seem to have been included under the general term *deutsch*. The
likeness of the Frisian to the Anglo-Saxon admitted of a certain
degree of intercourse, for the early Anglo-Saxon missionaries entered at once upon active labor on arriving in Frisia.[2]

Boniface is said to have spoken to his companions at the time of
the Frisian attack upon him in the speech of his own land, *patria
voce*, Anglo-Saxon. It is thus evident that work among the Frisians was based upon the acquisition of their language. It is as-
serted that the Frisians promised to receive the gospel, provided
Charlemagne would send to them some one who could speak their
own language, and Liudger, who was of Frisian birth, was sent
to them.[3] A general similarity between the languages of Ger-

---

[1] *Vita S. Bonifat*, Lib. II, c. 25.
[2] Wilfred labored a few months in 678 with great success.—*Vita S.
Wilfred in Acta SS. Bened.*, c. 25. Wigbert labored two years unsuc-
cessfully, from 690–692, owing to the opposition of their chief Radbod.
He was followed by Willebrord, bishop of Utrecht, A. D. 693; Adel-
bert, the patron saint of North Holland who founded the church in Eg-.
mont; Wulfram, bishop of Sens, 690; Boniface, 719–755, who was slain
at Dockum by the Frisians.
[3] Si eis aliquis deretur cujus loquelam intelligere possent.—*Vita S.
Liudgeri*, c. 16. Quoted by Mone, *Altniederländische Volksliteratur*,
p. 372.

many was early recognized. Thus it is said that all the barbarous nations living between the Rhine and the Weser, and between the Danube and the ocean, resemble each other in language, but in dress and custom are very dissimilar.[1] Augustine is said by Bede to have taken Frank interpreters with him to England from France (Gaul).[2]

Of national popular songs in Frisian there are no traces, and yet we have shown that the scene of Beowulf is partly on Frisian soil, and that Gudrun includes, mixed with its northern elements, many legendary events of Frisian history. There were Frisian bards, but their songs were never written and consequently have perished. In the life of St. Liudger we find that he met at Hellewird a blind singer, Bernlef, who sang of the deeds and conflicts of the ancient Frisian kings, and who was greatly beloved by the people.[3] These songs could only exist when the country was free from foreign influence, and where there was the bond of a national spirit and common history. The Frisian language has disappeared in North Holland, in East Frisia except in the Saterland, and in the districts of North Brabant, Drenthe, and Over-Yssel. In the west it has yielded to the Frankish or its modern representative, the Netherlandish, and in the east it has given way before the predominating political influence of the Saxon or Platt-deutsch. For 150 years the Frisians were constantly exposed to attacks from the Northmen. The last invasion occurred in 1010, when the Northmen entered Frisia and advanced into Holland. Frisia was given to the Norman chief Godfrey by Charles the Fat. Godfrey was soon assassinated, and Gerolf, the son of Theodore, a Count of Frisia, regained his hereditary domain. The Emperor Lewis gave Frisia to Herolt the Dane,[4] but the Norman dominion was always doubt-

---

[1] Omnesque praeterea barbaras nationes, quae inter Rhenum ac Wiseram fluvios oceanumque atque Danubium positae sunt, lingua quidem pene similes sed habitui vel moribus valde dissimiles, ita perdomuit ut eas sibi tributarias facerat.—*Pertz*, XI, 361. *Hist. Eccl. Ex. Hugo Floriacensis*, A. D. 1100.

[2] *Hist. Eccl.*, Lib. I, c. 25.

[3] Et ecce illo discumbente cum discipulis suis, oblatus est ei caecus vocabulo Bernlef, qui a vicinis suis valde diligebatur, eo quod esset affabilis et antiquorum actus regumque certamina bene noverat, psallendo promere. —*Vita S. Liud.*, Lib. II, c. 1, *Acta Benedict. Saec. IV*, p. 25.

[4] Tunc dominus imperator magnam partem Fresonam dedit ei [Heriolt de Danais]. Thegani—*Vita Hlud. Imp. Pertz*, II, 597. Frisia and Eng-

ful, and we cannot assume that the language was greatly affected during their uncertain supremacy. In the eleventh century Frisia, between the Lauwers and the Ems, passed under the temporal sovereignty of the bishops of Utrecht, and Frisia between the Ems and Weser became subject to the bishops of Bremen. During this period of incessant warfare and occasional temporary subjection to the Danes, perished probably all native literature, if any written memorials existed. Frisian chronicles speak of a magnificent temple at Stavoren, the seat of the Frisian kings, and of a long line of historical writers, among whom are mentioned Witho, the " wise," the chief of the Druids, who died A. D. 132 ; of Hanco Fortemannus, who lived in the time of Charlemagne and who wrote an account of his campaigns; of Sulco Fortemannus, who wrote a record of Frisian history from Frixo, the mythical founder of the race and brother of Aeneas, to Radbod II ; of Occo van Scharl, who lived in the tenth century, and who wrote the history of his time. Most of these statements rest on the authority of Suffridus Petri, who lived in the sixteenth century, and whose writings are marked by credulity and a love of romancing. There are no existing remains of the early language other than the words contained in the Lex Frisionum, and in the proper names contained in the monastic records.

An interesting fact which connects the earliest writings in the Frisian language with the writings of the other German nations, and which bears indirect witness to their age and authenticity, is the use of alliteration employed in their laws. Wiarda[1] called attention first to the alliterative character of these laws. He held the additions to them to be in part fragments of popular songs, poetic glosses, which gave to the people information regarding the origin and meaning of the laws.

In the second Küre in the Rustringer text we have:

Colnaburch hit by alda tidon	Cologne hight in olden times
Agrip anda alda noma;	And by olden name Agrip.
Tha firade us Frison	Then was strange to us Frisians
Thiu fire menote,	The foreign money,

---

land are said to have become subject to the Danes at the same time. Atque ex illo tempore Fresia et Anglia in ditione Danorum feruntur.—*M. Adami Gesta*, Lib. I, A. D. 876.

[1] *Asegabuch*, pp. 11, 167, 340.

And us swerade	And us inconvenienced,
Tha thi swera panning;	Then the heavy penny.
Setton tha selua	Set (established) we ourselves
Sundroge menote,	An especial coin,
And warth ther with thet	And there was with it,
Twa and siuguntich punda,	Two and seventy pounds,
Leyd and elagad,	Laid and valued,
Twa and siuguntichs killinga	Two and seventy shillings
Rednathes slekes ieftha	Of the stamp of Rednath, or
Kawinges slekes.	Of Kawing's stamp.
Rednath and Kawing	Rednath and Kawing.
Alsa hiton tha forma	So were hight the first,
Twene ther to Frislande	Two that in Friesland
Then pannig slogon.	The penny stamped.
Thriu pund tha frana,	Three pounds to the magistrate.
Thet ist en and twintich	That is one and twenty
Skillinga thruch thes Kyninges	
bon.	Shillings by the kings decree.

Of historical poems there are few traces. Lines appear which seem to have formed part of some Volkslied, as:

> " Hi was minnera
> And hi was betera
> Hi stifte and sterde
> Triwa and werde.
> And hi setta thera kenega ieft
> And allere liuda kest
> And landriucht
> And allera londa eccum sin riucht." [1]

Rask holds that these lines may have been taken from some poem relating to Charles Martel. Compare with these the following lines from a register of the kings who established good laws. [2]

Thesse fiuwer hera	These four lords
Bihulpon us	Helped us
Frison frihalses	Frisians to liberty
And fridomes,	And freedom
With thene kinig	With King Charles,
Kerl, hwanda alle	Because all

---

[1] *Rechtsquellen*, p. 343.
[2] *Ibid.* p. 133.

Frisa er north *h*erdon	Frisians to the north were subject,
Anda grimma *h*erna.	To the grim nations.

Rhyme appears later, and there are few traces of it in Frisian writings of unquestioned early date. Wiarda quotes as an example.[1]

Forth scele wi se halda,	Hereafter these will we keep,
And God scel urse walda,	And God shall rule o'er us,
Thes reddera and thes stitha	The weak and the strong,
And alle unriuchte thing formitha.	And all things wrong we will shun.

These lines form a conclusion to a gloss to the XVII Küren and the XXIV Landrechte in the Hunsingoer and Emsiger laws.

A rhymed poem of uncertain, but probably late date, contains the grant of special privileges made to the Frisians by Charlemagne.[2] The language of the poem does not differ much from the Hunsingoer text of the Kesta. The poem begins:

" Thit was to there stunde,
Tha the kening Kerl riuchta bigunde,
Tha waster ande there Saxinna merik,
Liudingerus en hera fele steric.[3]

Of glosses upon the Scriptures and translations into the Frisian, which form so large a part of early German literature, we find scarcely any traces, although in the laws of the different districts as well as in the ecclesiastical law (Sindriucht), there are constant provisions regarding priests, fasts, the sanctity of churches, obedience to spiritual authorities, etc. We have a fragment regarding the last judgment, also the ten commandments, with a sort of scriptural genealogy, to which is joined lists of the Roman emperors and of the early bishops who ruled over Frisia. The original dates of the rendering of these into Frisian cannot be determined, but the lists of kings who instituted wise laws is not earlier than the beginning of the fourteenth century. The earliest forms in the Frisian language are the words which occur in the Lex Frisionum.

---

[1] *Asegabuch*, p. 167. *Rechtsquellen*, p. 81.

[2] *Rechtsquellen*, p. 351.

[3] A Latin version of this charter is given by Schotanus.—*Beschrijvinge end Chronijck van Heerlickheydt von Frieslandt*, p. 64, 1655. Another copied from the state archives in Brussels is given in the Charterboek of Frisia, Vol. I, p. The Latin version was long held to be original, but its genuineness is no longer maintained.

LAWS IN LATIN.

DATE OF THE LEX FRISIONUM.

The earliest edition of the Lex Frisionum appeared in 1557 at Basel.[1] The law stands between the Lex Anglorum et Werniorum hoc est Thuringorum, and the Leges Burgundiorum. No original text of this law is known, and it is not known from what source Herold obtained the text which he used.[2] The editor states that for the Lex Salica he used a manuscript of Fulda, and that among those who contributed to this edition or aided in its collation were scholars of Basel, Milan and Worms. Herold speaks in one place of Saxmundus, one of the authors of the Additio Sapientum, as living in 600 A. D. Siccama assigns the collection of the laws to the time of Clothaire II, 613–628, or to his son Dagobert 628–638. Richthofen, however, with better reason, divides the laws into three parts, each of which he assigns to a different period. He holds that the oldest part was compiled after the subjugation of Frisia by the Franks under Charles Martel, in 734, and that it was in force in Central Frisia either during his reign or that of his son Pippin, 741. The second part of the law was in force throughout all Frisia after the conquest of East Frisia by Charlemagne, 785.

The third part or the Additio Sapientum, by which the provisions of the law were changed and differently applied, is subsequent to the year 802. The historical considerations which determine the date of these laws may be briefly given. The laws are in Latin, with many Frisian words. None of the laws of the German nations were written down until after the introduction of Christianity. With the single exception of the Anglo-Saxon laws, these laws were all written first in Latin. Dagobert I founded a Christian church at Utrecht on the borders of Frisia. The city was captured by the Frisian king Radbod and the church destroyed. The bishop of Cologne claimed jurisdiction over Utrecht in consequence of the

---

[1] Originum ac Germanicarum Antiquitatum Libri. Opera Basilii Ioannis Herold. Basiliae, 1557.

[2] Richthofen, in his edition of the Lex Frisionum, republished under the auspices of the Frisian Society, has refuted the theory of Gaupp that Lindenbrog in his edition of 1613, and Siccama, in his edition of 1617, used a manuscript original, by showing that these editions add nothing to the first edition of Herold. Huydecoper, in his edition of the Rijm Cronijk of Melis Stoke, Leiden, 1772, vol. I, 142, has doubted the genuineness of these laws. But a more complete study and a comparison with the laws of other German nations has established their genuineness.

chapel founded there by Dagobert, the ruins of which were discov-
ered by Willebrord, which belonged to the diocese of Cologne.[1] At
the period of the earliest missionary efforts in the seventh century,
Frisia was an independent kingdom free from Frankish dominion.
Anglo-Saxon missionaries had a transient tolerance there under
Adegild, and even later under Radbod, the most determined sup-
porter of Frisian liberty and of his ancestral religion.

After Radbod's death in 719, Western Frisia or Frisia west of the
Fli, came under the dominion of the Franks. Central Frisia retained
longer its practical independence and it was not subdued by Charles
Martel until 734. Still the people held obstinately to their old
heathenism, and in 755 the Archbishop Boniface was slain by them
at Dockum. Beyond the Lauwers all was pagan.[2] Charlemagne
entered this region A. D. 780,[3] and it was not until 785 that it was
fully subdued.

West Frisia was therefore subject to the Franks from 697 to 734.
West and Central Frisia from 734, and West, Central and East
Frisia from 785. We must therefore ascribe the extension of these
uniform laws to these periods. Only when the whole country had
come under the control of one sovereign could a uniform code of
laws have been prepared. Within this period and the reign of
Charlemagne we fix the date of the Lex Frisionum. The Norman
invasions began immediately subsequent to this, and continued

---

[1] Coloniensis episcopus dicit sedem Utraiectinam ad se pertinere, propter fundamenta cuiusdam destructae a paganis ecclesiolae, quam Wille-
brordus dirutam usque ad solum in castello Traiecto referit, et repert
quia ab antiquo rege Francorum Dagoberto castellum Traiectum cum
destructa eccelesia ad Coloniensen parociam donatum fuisse. Letter of
Boniface to Pope Stephen, ı. D. 754.—*Van Mieris, Charterboek.* The
statement of Richthofen that the Frisians and Franks lived at peace from
689–714 is not quite correct, as in 694 Pippin invaded and overran Frisia.
Pippinus dux Ratbodum ducem Fresonum bellando vicit Fresiamque
sibi subiugavit.—*Annal., Xant.* 655-714, *Pertz,* II, 220.
[2] Lagbeki ubi confinium erat christianorum ac paganorum cunctis diebus, Pippini regis.—*Vita S. Greg. Acta. Bened. Saec.* IV, p. 295.
[3] Carolus iterum ingreditur Saxoniam . . . et Windorum, seu et Fri-
sorum at Nordlandorum multitudo credidit.—*Annal. Lobiens, Pertz,*
II, 195. See also *Vita S. Willehad, Pertz.* II, 391. *Chron. Moissiacen,*
A. D. 787, and *Vita S. Liud,* Lib. II, 25.
   Hinc Carolus primus Frisonum marte magister,
   Pingitur et secum grandia gesta manus.
   —*Ermwold Nigel.,* Lib. IV, A. D. 826, *Pertz,* II, 506.

from 834 [1] to 1024 A. D., and anything like the compilation of a general code of laws would have been during this period impossible.

Later, during the reign of Lewis the Pious, these laws could not have received form, as various provinces of Frisia had been given to the leading Norman chiefs. It is impossible that any law embracing in any respect similar provisions, could at that time have originated and been applied to a country so divided and under so varying governments. Certain specifications regarding the amounts of fines and indemnities, the rules of proceedure, the relations of the moneys specified, lead to assign one portion of these laws to the period between 734–785,[2] a second portion to the period succeeding the conquest of East Frisia by Charlemagne, hence after 785, and the third portion to the general examination and codification of all the laws of the different tribes at Aachen in 802.

The term *ewa* for law appears first in an early record of 855, already quoted, in which property in Hamaland is conveyed according to the law of the Salian and Ripuarian Franks, *nec non secundum ewa Fresonum.* Many provisions in the Lex Frisionum are unquestionably of remote heathen origin. The law recognizes ancient national customs (Gewohnheitsrecht) continued beside the recognized common law or Volksrecht. All distinctively pagan features are removed from the law, save a single passage which has given rise to much controversy. It provides that whoever shall violate a shrine and carry away any of the sacred objects, shall be conducted to the shore of the sea, and that there his ears shall be slit and he shall be sacrificed to the gods whose temple he has violated. This occurs under Title XI of the Additio Sapientum, given by Wulemarus one of the revisers.[2] His name shows him to have been a Frisian.[3]

---

[1] This is the earliest mention I find of a Norman invasion. Interim etiam classis de Danis veniens in Frisiam aliquam partem ex illo devastavit, et per Vetus-Traiectum ad emporium quod vocatur Dorestadus, venientes omnia diripuerunt.—*Annal., Bert. Pertz,* I, 428.

[2] *Richthofen,* p. XLI.

[3] Hoc trans Laubachi de honore templorum. Qui fanum effregit et ibi aliquid de sacris tulerit, ducitur ad mare et in sabulo quod accessus maris operire solet, finduntur aures eius et castratur et immolatus diis quorum templa violavit.

This seems to be more the statement of a custom than a law. The subjunctive would have been used in the verbs *ducatur* and *immoletur* were it any other than a mere note written by some reviser, as Richthofen suggests.

After Charlemagne had been crowned in Rome A. D. 800,[1] he observed the defects in the laws of the different tribes under his dominion, and that provisions of law even among the Salian and Ripuarian Franks were often dissimilar. He therefore sought to remedy these deficiencies by the addition of *Capitula*—special brief statements which removed any inconsistency, and yet left the substance of the law unchanged. The laws of the different tribes were reduced to writing, and it was even directed that national songs commemorating the deeds of their kings should be preserved. In the year 802, at a great council of princes, nobles, clergy and jurists, these laws were read before the emperor and translated.[2] Emendations were made, and the law as amended was written down in order that "judges might administer justice according to that which was written, and not receive bribes."[3] Later to wise and learned men was entrusted an examination into the operations and results of these laws.[4] All defects were to be reported to the

---

[1] Post susceptum imperiale nomen, cum adverteret multa legibus populi sui deesse, nam Franci duas habent leges in plurimis locis valde diversas, cogitavit quae deerant addere et discrepantia unire, prava quoque ac perperam prolata carrigere : sed de his nihil aliud ab eo factum, nisi quod pauca capitula et ea imperfecta legibus addidit. Omnium tamen nationum quae sub eius dominatu erant, iuraque scripta non erant describere ac literis mandari facit. Item barbara et antiquissima carmina quibus veterum regum actus et bella canebantur, scripsit et memoriaeque mandavit. Inchoavit et grammaticam patrii sermonis.—*Einhardi, Vita Caroli M.* § 29.

[2] Sed et imperator interim, quod ipsum synodum factum est, congregavit duces comites et reliquo Christiano populo cum legislatoribus, et fecit omnes leges in regno suo legi et tradi, unicuique homini legem suam et emendare, ubicumque necesse fuit, et emendatam legem scribere, et ut judices per scriptum judicassent et munera non accepissent.—*Annal., Lauresh*, A. D. 802. *Pertz, Mon. Ger. SS.* I, 38.

[3] The laws of the Frisians, Thuringians, Salian and Ripuarian Franks, and of the Chamavi are supposed to have been reduced to writing at this time.

[4] Karolus elegit ex optimatibus suis prudentissimis et sapientissimis viros tam archiepiscopis quam et reliquis episcopis, simulque et abbates venerabiles laicosque religiosos, et direxit in universum reguum suum et per eos cunctis subsequentibus secundum rectam legem vivere concessit. Ubi autem aliter quam recte et juste in lege aliquit esse constitutum, hoc diligentissimo animo exquirere jussit et sibi innotescere, quod ipse, donante Deo, meliorare cepit ut longa consuetudo, quae ad utilitatem publicam non impendit, pro lege servetur et quae diu servatae sint, permanent. Capit. A. D. 813, c. 17. Volumus ut hommes talem consuetudinem habent sicut antiquitus Longobardorun fuit, A. D. 823, c. 14.—*Pertz, SS.* I, 193.

emperor for adjustment. Long standing national custom was to be retained and to have equal force with written law, unless there was a conflict between them, when the written law was to be followed. *Ewa* was equivalent to a law embodying national usage, (Gewohnheitsrecht).

The Lex Frisionum consists of two parts, the law proper and the Additio Sapientum. The former is divided into twenty-two titles, each embracing many separate specifications; the latter contains eleven titles and also many separate specifications. Penalties are specified with great fullness and exactness, for murder, theft, violence, mismarriage, unchastity, incendiarism, violation of oaths, indemnity for injuries and personal affronts. In many cases the number of the witnesses or judicial supporters (Eideshelfer) of the accused are given. Penalties are assessed not merely according to the rank of the injured, but according to that of the transgressor. These are estimated in money of different coinages, old and new. The fines are uniform throughout Frisia only in a few cases. The three divisions of Frisia, each of which had in part an independent legal status are mentioned. The home of Frisian law was unquestionably Central Frisia, and variations for the other districts from the legal requirements here, are specified in notes.

If the law does not denote definitely for what district its statement holds, the preface indicates for entire Frisia or the special division to which it applies. If the passage relates to the central part, short remarks specify the penalties and the oath-helpers for the other parts. Only one passage of the revisers, Wlemarus and Saxmundus, is incorporated in the text.[1] This may show contemporary revision. The penalties in the law and in the Additio do not correspond. For bodily injuries they are increased threefold.[2] That the laws were composed under the reign of the Frankish kings is evident from the use the titles, of king and duke, side by side; also from the payment of the *fredum* or peace mony to the king. There are no traces of Roman law in the Lex Frisionum and the influence of other tribal laws cannot be certainly shown.

Certain penalties for bodily injuries are the same in the Lex Fri-

---

[1] At the end of Tit. II, § 10.
[2] See *Wilda, Strafrecht der Deutschen*, 618–622. De Geer holds that these enactments were made in the tenth and eleventh centuries.—*Over de Zamenstelling van de Lex Frisionum*, pp. 189–195.

sonum and the Lex Anglorum. Once the enactment is said to be from the king.[1]

THE RELATION OF THE FRISIANS TO THE ANGLES AS SUGGESTED IN THE LEX FRISIONUM.

It has been attempted to determine a connection between the Angles and the Frisians, by a comparison of the Lex Frisionum with the Lex Anglorum et Werniorum hoc est Thuringorum. The latter code is undoubtedly old in substance, but in the form in which we possess it has been subject to revision.[2] The law exhibits no traces of Christian influence and ideas, and evidently has its origin in times of pure paganism. The frequent mention of the duel in it is especially noticeable. It has been held to have originated in Schleswig, in a district on the Maas called Thuringia or Thoringia, and in the present Thuringia in Central Germany. It must have originated in a district where Frisian and Frankish forms were mixed both in the laws as well as in the language.[3] The Frankish element predominates. There is great similarity to the Lex Chamavorum.

According to Zoepfl,[4] the law may have received its name either because it originated in Thuringia or was carried to Denmark by way of North Thuringia. Some form of this law was carried to England, where it bore the name Lex Werniorum et Thuringorum. The term Anglorum was dropped, as applying to the laws of the Angles, which originated on English soil.

In the Constitutiones de Foresta of Canute a fine is assessed according to the law of the Werni and Thuringians.[5] It is suggested

---

[1] The laws of only two tribes seem to have emanated from their kings, those of the Longobards under king Rothari 636–652 A. D., and those of the Anglo-Saxons. Titles I, III, §§ 1–7; IV, §§ 1–8; IX, §§ 1–3, are held to belong to the old national law (Volksrecht). Titles II, V, XI, XIV, to previous unwritten custom-law, Gewohnheitsrect. Frankish enactments in Frisia are shown in III, §§ 8, 7; IX, §§ 14–17.

[2] *Gaupp, Das Alte Gesetz der Thüringer.*

[3] See H. Müller. Der Lex Salica und der Lex Anglorum et Werniorum Alter und Heimath, § 19; also Merkel, Lex Salica, Nachtrag in Lex Saxonum 1853.—Gengler's Germanische Rechtsdenmäler, p. 166.

[4] *Deut. Rechtsgeschichte*, p. 51.

[5] Et emendet secundum pretium hominis mediocris, quod secundum legem Werniorum, *i. e.*, Thuringorum, est ducentorum solidorum Qui liberum occiderit C. C. solidos componat.—*Schmidt, Gesetze der Angelachsen* p. 321. Also Lex Anglorum et Werniorum, I, § 1.

that king Harold to whom had been given a district north of the Elbe,[1] carried this law to Schleswig-Holstein, the early home of the Angles.[2] He is said to have given laws and statutes to those who dwelt across the Elbe, as well as the Frisians.

Whether the Lex Noricorum et Danorum, which it is claimed prevailed in the north of France, was carried thence to England may be questioned. The Lex Salica and the Lex Ripuaria certainly influenced early English law, and penalties are specified based upon provisions in these laws.[3] Danish law prevailed in Norfolk, Suffolk and Kent, and William the Conqueror confirmed this law and directed its general enforcement as being nobler than the laws of the British tribes.[4] This was based on a general resemblance between the Lex Noricorum or Norwegensium and the Lex Danorum.[5]

That a Thoringia existed on the right bank of the Rhine, we have that statement of Gregory of Tours, who in speaking of the crossing of that river by the Franks, says: "Many affirm that the Franks settled first on the shores of the Rhine, which they afterwards crossed and passed through Thoringia, where they elected kings to rule over them from the families of the nobles." Chlogio is said to have been king of the Franks, whose camp or citadel was at Dispargum, on the borders of Thoringia.[6]

---

[1] Et quia interdum pacifice in regno suo Herioldus rex consistere non poterat, dedit ei memoratus Augustus (Hludowicus) ultra Albiam beneficium, ut si quando ei necessarium esset ibi subsistere possit.—*Vita S. Anskarii*, c. 8, 9.

[2] (Haroldus) transalbianis et Fresonum genti leges et jura constituit, quae adhuc pro tanti anctoritate viri servare et contendunt.—*Albert, Stad.* A. D. 983.

[3] In the laws of Henry I are found various penalties prescribed according to these laws. "Secundum legem Saligam," c. 87, § 10; also c. 89, § 1; also "secundum legem Ribuariorum solvatur," c. 90, § 4.— *Schmidt*, pp. 482, 485.

[4] Erat etiam Lex Danorum in Northfolc at Suthfolc at Cantibrigesire, . In omnibus aliis causis et forisfacturis eandem legem habitant cum supradictis Norwensibus. Quam cum rex Willielmus audisset, cum aliis sui regni legibus maxime appretiatus est eam, et praecepit ut observaretur per universum regnum. Proferebat enim . . . quod antecessores ejus de Norweja olim venissent, et hac auctoritate leges eorum cum praedictis Danorum, et regni sui legibus asserebat debere sequi et observare.— *Leges Edw. Confess.*, c. 33, 34.

[5] Stobbe asserts that there is no proof that Canute carried the Danish law to England, and that under the name Lex Danorum the Lex Thuringorum is to be understood.—*Rechtsgeschichte*, 1860.

[6] Tradunt enim multi eosdem primum quidem litora Rheni amnis in-

Childerich fled to Basinus, in the neighborhood of the Scheldt. This Thoringia must have been in the neighborhood of the sea, as Basina says: "in transmarinis partibus aliquem cognovissem utiliorem te." Chlodwig made war on the Thoringians and brought them under his dominion. He was separated from the present Thuringia by intervening tribes. The Thuringians are frequently joined with the inhabitants of Brabant, in the early epics, as in that of king Rother, 4829.[1]

"Dorringen unde Brâbant, Vriesen unde Hollant,
Gaf he vier hêren, die mit ime wâren
Uzir lande gevarin."

Sahsen und Turinge, Plîsum und Swurven
Gaf he zên graven,

where Thuringia adjacent to Holland, Friesland and Brabant is meant.

In the Traveler's Tale two Thuringias—Thyringas and Eâstþyringas[2]—are mentioned.

Historical notices of the Werni place them in the centre of Germany near the Angles,[3] who reside as far east of the Longobards as the centre of the river Elbe.[4]

Procopius[5] places the Werni later on the shores of the Rhine, near the mouth. Here they were associated with the Angles and the Suevi.[6] The Angles and the Suevi are associated in the Traveler's

coluisse, dehinc, transacto Rheno, Thoringiam transmeasse. Ferunt etiam tunc Chlogionem utilem ac nobilissimum in gente sua regem Francorum fuisse, qui apud Dispargum castrum habitabat, quod est in termino Thoringorum.—*Greg. of Tours*, 2, 9.
1 Quoted by *Grimm, Ges. der dent. Spr.*, p. 417, 3d ed.
2 Lines 320, 17; 322, 16 and 323, 30. Quoted by *Grimm*, 42.
2 *Tacitus, Ger.* 40. Reudigni deinde et Aviones et Anglii et Varini fluminibus aut silvis muniuntur.
4 Τῶν δὲ ἐντὸς καὶ μεσογείων ἐθνῶν μέγιστα μέν ἐστι τό τε τῶν Σουήβων τῶν Ἀγγειλῶν οἵ εἰσιν ἀνατολικώτεροι τῶν Λαγγοβάρδων ἀνατείνοντες πρὸς τὰς ἄρκτους μέχρι μέσων τῶν τοῦ Ἄλβιος ποταμοῦ, καὶ τὸ τῶν Σουήβων τῶν Σεμνόνων οἵτινες διήκουσι μετὰ τὸν Ἄλβιν ἀπὸ τοῦ εἰρημένου μέρους πρὸς ἀνατολὰς μέχρι τοῦ Σουήβου ποταμοῦ. —*Ptol.*, Lib. II, XI.
5 4, 20.
6 The early name of Zeeland may come from Suevi, Zeewen. It is possible that the Frisians formed a part of the great southern migration

Tale, *Engle* and *Swaefe*. Traces of the Werni appear in the name Weringouwe, a district on the Werra, and possibly in Warmond, the name of a village near Leiden.[1]

Traces of the onward march of the Angles to the sea are found in the term Engilgowe, on the Unstrut in Thuringia, Engelen in North Brabant, Hengeloo in Gelderland, and Over-Yssel, and in the Pays de l'Angle in West Flanders, near Burburg, as well as in Angeln, between the bays of Flensburg and Kiel in Schleswig. It remains for us to assume a double movement of the Angles proceeding from Thuringia, one to the north along the Elbe and terminating in the present Angeln on the Baltic, and a second down the Rhine to the sea, or as Grimm asserts[2] from the north up the Elbe and thence to the Weser. Anglo-Saxon records unite in placing the home of the Angles who invaded England on the peninsula of Schleswig-Holstein and the islands of the Baltic Sea to the East.[3] It cannot be doubted that they occupied a great extent of coast, and hence their migration in large numbers was to be expected. The Frisians are mentioned as one of the three nations which settled England, the others being the Angles and the Britons.[4]

In what proportions these different tribes contributed to the population and to the language of England, it is impossible to determine. It is certain that the Frisians in England at no time existed as a separate political unit in the people or government.

---

of nations, and settled with the Suevi in Switzerland, according to a national tradition.

[1] Grimm and Latham point to a possible relation between the words Werni, and Werra and Weser.

[2] *Grimm*, p. 421.

See the Anglo-Saxon Chronicle, A. D. 449; King Alfred's Orosius, Book I, c. 1; Bede, Hist. Eccl., Lib. I, c. XV.

[3] Βριττίαν δὲ τὴν νῆσον ἔθνη τρία πολυανθρωπότατα ἔχουσι, βασιλεύς τε εἰς αὐτῶν ἑκάστῳ ἐφέστηκεν, ὀνόματα δὲ κεῖται τοῖς ἔονεσι τούτοις Ἀγγίλοι τε καὶ Φρίσσονες καὶ οἱ τῇ νήσῳ ὁμωνόμενοι Βρίττονες.—*Procopius, De Bello Gothico*, Lib. IV, c. 19.

I. LAWS WRITTEN IN FRISIAN.

These were not composed by the people, but by their judges or representatives, in general assemblies. In content they relate to the most varied domain of law. They contain, like the Lex Frisionum, carefully detailed statements of the personal rights of individuals and the laws of property with penalties for their violation. The Frisian laws, like the Anglo-Saxon, bear the name *domar*,[1] judicial decrees also *kesta* or *liudkesta*,[2] that is, laws enacted by the popular will, (Willküren). Single laws bear the name landriuchta (landrechte), or common law of the country. The ecclesiastical law[3] is also specially defined in distinction from this, so also is the law proceeding from the emperor. The distinction prevailing elsewhere in Germany, between *landrecht* and *lehnrecht* is seldom made,[4] that between national, the common law of the land, and city law (Stadtrecht) appears later.

GENERAL LAWS IN FORCE THROUGHOUT ALL FRISIA.

1. The Seventeen Kesta of the twelfth century. These are preserved in Latin (Petitiones), Frisian and Low German versions. They contain provisions relating to the tenure of real estate, coinage, records of judicial proceedings, proof, military service, the preservation of the peace, bodily injuries. In many cases reference is made to enactments or special grants of Charlemagne. To the body of the laws are added *Wenden* or exceptions. Manuscripts written in the Hunsingoer, Emsiger and Rustringer dialects are preserved.

2. The Twenty-four Landriuchta. These were composed before 1252 A. D., and treat of landed property and of its alienation, inheritance, crime, blood-revenge, indemnity for injuries, etc. The stat-

---

[1] Nu aegh di grewa dine Asega toe bannane toe een riuchta doem.— *Rechtsquellen, Wester-lawers Laws*, p. 4, 2, 6. Hyr bigannath thar domar ther alle Amsgane bi riuchtat.—*Emsiger Laws*, p. 194, 1.

[2] Brocmen kiasath thet to enre kere.—*Laws of the Brocmen*, p. 173, 24. Tha ur ief us thi kinig Kerl, sa hwer sa alle liode enne kere kere. Tha keron Riostringa tha kera.—*Laws of the Rustringer*, p. 115, 2, 5.

[3] Sineth- (synod) riuchta and landriucht.—*Hunsingoer Laws*, p. 342, 34. Ney riochta keysersriocht ende landriocht.—*Urkunde of* 1374. *Rechtsquellen*, p. 560, 12.

[4] Wirth aeck ean kynd stom of blynd of fuetlos of handloes berren dat mey eerfnama wessa, ney na landriucht ende naet ney leenriucht. A child born dumb or blind, or without hands or feet, may not receive an inheritance, neither according to feudal nor national law.

ates use in part the XVII Kesta. The characterization is broad and poetic. Later these laws were included in the special laws of the seven Seelands.[1]

3. The General Boetregisters or classifications of fines of about the same date as the preceding. These contain penalties for various criminal offenses.

4. The additional Kesta or Ueberküren. These are seven in number and are of the thirteenth century. They are preserved in a Hunsingoer and Emsiger Frisian, and in a Low German version; also in a later form, but we cannot determine in what district they originated.

5. The Upstallbomer laws of 1323. These were not in force east of the Ems. They consist of resolutions or enactments of representatives of the seven Seelands, consisting of grietmen, magistrates, bishops and clergy,[2] who met yearly at Upstallbom, near Aurich. These occur in a Frisian and in a longer Latin version. Seven additional propositions were added in an assembly at Groningen, in the year 1361, which were to be in force for six years. They contain an agreement for mutual assistance in case of attack, also special penalties for crimes, to be enforced throughout the seven Seelands.

II. THE LAWS OF SINGLE COMMUNITIES OR STATES.

Frisia at our earliest acquaintance with it was divided in separate

---

[1] The seven Seelands are described in a document of the fifteenth century. The first, West Frisia, the present North Holland, embracing Horn, Enkhuizen, and Medemblik, which became early subject to the counts of Holland; the second, the district east of the Flie between Stavoren and Leeuwarden, including Westergo; the third, Ostergo—the east half of the present province of Friesland, between the Borne and thè Lauwers; the fourth, Drenthe, which became subject to the bishops of Utrecht, and the south western part of the present province of Friesland; the fifth included the district about Groningen between the Lauwers and the Ems; the sixth, the country along the coast between the Weser and the Elbe; the seventh, the country of the Rustringers and the land to the north of the Elbe, possibly extending to the Eider and including the Strand or North Frisians. The map of Alting is his Notitia Germaniae Inferioris Antiquae, 1698 A. D., differs greatly from this account.

[2] Grietmanni, iudices, praelati et clerus terrarum, Oestergoe et Westergoe, cum caeteris Zelandiis.—*Rechtsquellen*, p. 102.
These assemblies ceased to be held early in the thirteenth century, but were resumed in A. D. 1323.

parts by natural boundary lines of river and lakes. In the life of Boniface it is said that he visited the country of the Frisians, which was divided into many separate districts, which though called by different names yet are occupied by one race.[1] These laws were occasionally enacted by delegates from two states in common session, as in statutes of the Brocmen and Emsigers.[2]

I. THE LAWS OF THE RUSTRINGER.

These were in force in the district of Rustri, west of the mouth of the Weser in the present Oldenburg. Manuscripts in Frisian of the thirteenth century, also in Netherlandish of the fourteenth and fifteenth centuries, exist. They contain keran or kesta, new keran, a boetregister or list of fines, judicial decrees, a statement of taxes due the priests, etc. (*Priester Bothe*), said to have been authorized by Charlemagne and Pope Leo, a sendbrief or in part ecclesiastical charter containing a statement of the authority and prerogatives of the Archbishop of Bremen, also obligations due the church ascribed to Charlemagne, Leo and Bishop Willehad, a·fragment relating to the Last Judgment and the Ten Commandments. Connected with these is a list of the kings who have established law. These laws joined to the general Frisian laws, have been called arbitrarily by Wiarda, the Asegaboek or the book of the judges.

2. Laws in force among the Brocmen, a district in the neighborhood of Aurich. These contain two series of Kesta in Latin, enacted jointly by the Brocmen and the Emsigers, a Latin sendbrief of the year 1251, a treaty or reconciliation between the Bishop of Münster and the four districts of Brockmerland, Emsigerland, Reiderland and Alombechta (or Oldcampt). of 1276 in Latin, Frisian and Netherlandish, and the Brocmerbrief which is closely related to the Emsiger Pfenningschuldsbuch of the thirteenth century.

3. The laws in force in Emsigerland, the region of Emden. These contain the Emsiger Domar of 1312, which are preserved in Latin and in two Frisian texts, also in Netherlandish; the so-called Pfennigschuldbuch from *pannengskelde* with which is begins. It

---

[1] Autemque paganam Fresonum visitavit quae interea centibus aquis in multos agrorum dividitur pagos ita ut diversis appellati nominibus unius tamen gentis proprietatem portendunt (protendunt).—*Vita S. Bonifat,* c. 34, A. D. 755.

[2] Statuerunt iudices Brocmanine et Emesgonie.—*Rechtsquellen,* p. 137.

treats of debt, inheritance, private rights, penalties, a Fiaeid[1] and the methods of ecclesiastical courts or judgments.

4. The laws of Westerwold, a district west of the Ems and south of Winschoten, in the present province of Groningen. These consist of a landrecht of 1470, together with a later revision of the same in 1567, confirmed by Philip II and Margaret of Parma. This is perhaps the latest of the whole body of Frisian laws.

5. The laws of Fivelgo, a province north east of the city of Groningen and west of the Ems. A considerable portion of these laws are only found in Latin and Netherlandish versions. They are in great variety and are often enactments in common of the provinces of Hunsingo and Fivelgo. They contain provisions relating to criminal law, and several relating to inheritance. The Appingdammerbrief was enacted by delegates from all Frisia at Upstallbom in 1327.

6. The laws of Hunsingo, a district east of the Hunse river, north of Groningen on the coast, extending to the mouth of the Ems. These contain Kesta of 1252, possibly from a Latin original, the Ten Commandments, the Five Keys of Wisdom, list of kings who established law, also the rhymed charter of Frisian liberty from Charlemagne, undoubtedly of late origin,[2] and a list of penalties (Boetregister). The other laws of the fourteenth century are in Latin and Netherlandish.

7-9. The Laws of Humsterland, between the Hunse and the Lauwers, northwest of the city of Groningen, of Langewold, east of the Lauwers and south of Humsterland, and of Fredewold south of Langewold and west of Groningen in the province of Groningen.

---

[1] The nature of this oath is uncertain. Grimm considers it an oath taken upon money marked with a cross.—*Rechtsalterthümer*, p. 907. In another case it seems to be an oath taken by a woman on the threshhold of her home, accused of the concealment of some portion of her husband's estate.—*Rechtsquellen*, 166, 18. It was also taken in certain cases of bodily injury.

[2] The genuineness of the bull of 802, given by Charlemagne, granting to the Frisians perpetual liberty is extremely doubtful. It exists in various forms in Latin and Low German. That some such grant was made can scarcely be doubted, as it is referred to in the charter confirming the rights and privileges of the Frisians given by king William at Aachen in 1248.—*Charterboek*, I, 94. This rhymed version is probably the expression of a national tradition, but elaborated to enforce the popular belief in freedom from foreign dominion in the sixteenth century.—*Rechtsquellen*, p. 351.

These are of the thirteenth century, and are only preserved in Netherlandish versions from Latin originals.

10. The laws of Friesland, west of the Lauwers, the present province of Frisia. This district is to be regarded as the earliest and the most permanent abode of the Frisians. It was divided into three parts—Ostergo, the district between the Lauwers and Borne, embracing the neighborhood of Dockum and Leeuwarden; Westergo, between the Borne and the Flie, and including the region of Franeker, Harlingen, Bolsward and Stavoren; and Sevenwolden, a narrow tract south of Ostergo and Westergo, between Drenthe and the Zuider-Zee. This collection is very extensive.

The laws are of two kinds: general, extending over the whole district of Friesland west of the Lauwers; and, special, relating to particular provinces. The general laws contain numerous specifications regarding the authority of the count or deputy who administised justice (Schulzenrecht) in the emperor's name, and of the Asega or judge. The laws include provisions regarding Wergeld, Marktrecht, a criminal code of the year 1276, enactments regarding coinage. the so-called Emperor Rudolph's book, containing statements of law mixed with reflections and historical references, a treatise on "What is law?", a fragment regarding Charles Martel and the Frisian king Radbod, also the Kesta of Magnus.

The special laws contain in additional to the general provincial laws, the laws of certain local districts. The most of these laws are of the fourteenth and fifteenth centuries.

IV. The meagre remains of laws in force in the province of Drenthe are only preserved in Latin and Netherlandish.

V. Laws of the North Frisians, residing north of the Eider along the coast of Schleswig and on the adjacent islands.

1. For the southern portion of North Frisia, embracing the region of Eiderstedt, Utholm, and Everschop are preserved laws dating from 1418 to 1446.

2. Of laws relating to the northern part of North Frisia there exists the Siebenhardenbeliebung. This is a brief code of twenty-three paragraphs enacted on the island of Föhr in 1426, by seven communities, residing in part on the North Frisian islands, and in part on the adjacent coast. The language of all these laws of North Frisia is more nearly Low German than Frisian.

Of Frisian laws in force in North Holland we have no remains.

This region became subject to the courts of Holland in the eleventh century

The oldest manuscripts of any portion of the Frisian laws are not probably earlier than the fourteenth century, that of the Rustringer laws preserved in the grand ducal library at Oldenburg, is of about the year 1300. A copy of the Rustringer Busstaxen of 1327 A. D. is preserved in the grand ducal library at Hanover. A parchment manuscript of the laws of the Broemen of 1345, is also contained in the same library. A parchment manuscript of the Hunsingoer laws of about 1400 is preserved at Leeuwarden. Two charters exist with the original seals still upon them, one of 1374 at Franeker, and one of 1390, at Leeuwarden.

Among the literary remains which belong to what may be termed the middle period of Frisian literature, and which deserve mention as memorials of the language, are two works called *Thet Freske Riim* and the *Gesta Fresonum*. The Freske Riim was written in Frisian, but translated from the Latin of a certain Master Alwijn, who was rector of the Latin School at Sneek about 1400. Alwijn was learned in Roman law and church history. His title of Master was received from some foreign university. His narrative begins with the Creation, rambles through sacred and profane history, through lives of Jewish patriarchs and Roman kings. His Frisians served in Asia the king of heaven, but sailed to Europe and were enslaved and forced to become idolators by a Danish king. The poem, which is but a fragment when compared with the existing Netherlandish version, contains 1671 unequal rhymed lines. The poem was evidently divided at first into separate parts, each bearing a special title, as the "Rhyme of Noah and his Child," etc. The narration is tame and spiritless. The rhyme is monotonous from the repetition of the same final words. The language is in the main pure, and the forms, those of Frisia west of the Lauwers.

The Gesta Fresonum is a translation into Frisian of a prose narrative called the Gesta Frisiorum, written in Netherlandish in the latter part of the fifteenth century. A rhymed history written in the same language, called the "Olde Freesche Cronike," also exists. Both point to an earlier Latin original. The same events are related in both in about the same terms, but in a different order. The original author drew from the legends of St. Lebuinus, of Boniface and Liudger, the Bishop's Book of Utrecht and a Saxon and Frisian chronicle. The author was a Frisian who resided at Utrecht not later than 1474. The subject of this work is the usual mingling of scriptural and early mythical Frisian history with the lives of the saints. The blending of Saxon and Frisian legends is manifest in all these early chronicles. The brothers Saxo, Bruno and Friso sail from an island in India, called "Frisia the Blest," where St. Thomas had preached. They reach the coast of Europe; Saxo settles on the Elbe, and becomes the ancestor of the Saxons; Bruno resides on the Weser and founds Brunswick; Friso settles Frisia, and gives to his seven sons the Seven Seelands. A daughter, Wijmolt, resided on the east of the Weser and gave her name to the country, which embraced Ditmarsh. There is an echo here of the story of Hildeburg in Beowulf. The order of narration is confused and inconsequential. The language is not entirely pure, and the influence of Netherlandish forms is manifest.

THE LANGUAGE.

Upon the west, the Frankish in its present representative the Netherlandish, has supplanted the Frisian in North Holland. Of the language spoken in West Frisia between the Scheldt and the Flie, there are no remains except those left in a few proper names and early records, and it is not possible to determine the dialect of Frisian which was spoken there. The language was spoken as late as the middle of the seventeenth century in the Waterland north of the IJ.[1] The pronunciation of the letters z, v and sch in North Holland is like that of the Frisian s, f and sk.[2] The political separation of the two portions of Frisia east and west of the Flie, was so great as to produce alienation and often warfare. The irruption of the ocean which produced the Zuider-Zee in the thirteenth century completed the separation. To the east the Saxon has occupied the whole of the district between the Weser and the Ems. In Groningen, Netherlandish is spoken. The East Frisian is a living language only amid the moors of Saterland on the Leda, and on the island of Wangeroog. Frisian is spoken at present in the province of Friesland, east of the Zuider-Zee. The language of the schools

---

[1] Over de Taal en de Tongvallen der Friezen.—*Winkler*, p. 11.
[2] *J. H. Halbertsma in the Vrije Fries*, vol. X, 346.

and the pulpit is however Netherlandish. In the cities and larger towns Frisian is scarcely heard. The language of the Bildt is old Netherlandish mixed with Frisian forms. The so-called city Frisian, *stadfriesch*, which hitherto prevailed in the larger towns as in Leeuwarden, Dockum, Bolsward, Franeker, Sneek and Harlingen is the language of the south of Holland of the fifteenth and sixteenth centuries. The dialect of Hendeloopen on the Zuider-Zee presents many old as well as unusual and strange forms, not contained in the other dialects.

On the north the Saxon has supplanted the Frisian in Ditmarsch, Eiderstedt and in the islands of Nordstand and Pellworm. Only in thirty-eight parishes of the three counties of Tondern, Bredstedt and Husum which lie on the west coast of Schleswig, and upon some islands and halligs of the North Sea is Frisian still spoken. The number of inhabitants in these districts does not exceed 30,000. Even here, there is a great variety of forms, expression and pronunciation. On the mainland, the language is purest in the Risum Moor and in the district south of Wiedau, along the coast to Bredstedt. The speech of the inhabitants of the islands of Föhr, except in the parish of Wijk, and on the islands of Sylt and Amrum is different from that of the mainland and can scarcely be understood there. The language is more ancient but ruder. The East Moringers use the dual of the personal and possessive pronoun where the West Moringers use the plural. The language here is free from both Low German and Danish elements.[1]

The language in which the Frisian laws were written presents several dialects with well defined lines of difference. Commencing at the east the Rustringer dialect, spoken west of the Weser in Oldenburg, has preserved the original forms of words most closely, and is to be taken as the basis of comparison with the other dialects and the Anglo-Saxon, Old Saxon and Norse. West of the Rustringer dialect is the speech of Brokmerland, in the neighborhood of Aurich; further to the west existed the speech of Emsigerland, the region of Emden, then the language of Fivelgo, a district west of the Ems; of Hunsingo, east of the Lauwers-Zee, and north of Groningen, extending along the coast of Westerlauwersches Friesland, and embracing the present province of Frisia; containing the two provinces of

---

[1] Die Nordfriesische Sprache nach der Moringer Mundart. —*Bendsen*, p. XXIII.

Ostergo and Westergo. The speech of Ostergo, most nearly re-
sembles the forms of the dialects to the east, while that of Westergo
presents the most variations from these dialects. The Fivelgoer dialect is nearest to the Frisian west of the Lauwers.

The External Relations of the Frisian Language.

The Frisian presents both in inflections and vocabulary greater resemblance to the Anglo-Saxon than to any other Germanic dialect.
It is less rich in inflections than the Anglo-Saxon, but exhibits far
greater facility and variety in the formation of compound words.
In forms of consonants it exhibits remarkable parallelism to the
modern English, not always in words as written but as pronounced.
The Frisian more nearly than any other dialect of Germany re-
sembles the Norse. Analogies are found in the nominative plural
of masculine nouns, which present two forms in *a* or *ar*, corresponding to the masculine and feminine nouns of the A-declension and
to the masculine of the weak declension in Icelandic. This form is
like the old High German *ir*, which is in that language limited to
neuter nouns. The infinitive of all verbs also ends in *a*, the *n* having been dropped.

The form assumed by the palatals *k* and *g* present a wide range
of analogy to the English, *k* before *e, i, ia* and *iu* in the umlaut becomes often *sz* or *sth, tz* or *ts*. This occasioned a series of parallel
forms of words existing beside the original form, as *kerke* (church)
sthereke, skiurke and *tsiurke*, in which the lingual aspirate *th* passes
into the lingual sibilant, modern Frisian *tjerke*. This change is
found in all the Frisian dialects. The Rustringer, however, shows
only the affricative and presents few examples of the simple palatal.
The other dialects all exhibit parallel forms as *ketel*, kittle, *szetel, tsetel,
tsietel; kerl*, churl, *tzerl*, modern Frisian *tzierl; kiasa*, choose,
tziesa; kise, cheese, *tzise*. In the inlaut of words the same change
appears as *lega*, lay, *ledsa, lidsia*, and *leia*, modern Frisian, *lidze;
breka*, break, part, *ebreken, ebreszen, bretsen, britsin*, modern Frisian, *britzin; strika*. stroke, *striza*, modern Frisian, *stritzen;* so also
dekke, deck, modern Frisian, *ditzen, stekke*, stick, *stitzen; sega*, say,
sidze.

In *weitsje*, wake, *reitsje*, rake, *loaitsje*, look, this change has taken
place in the present tense while the participle retains the palatal *k*,
as *wekke, rekke, lôkke*.

The range of analogy is far greater in modern Frisian and modern English, even than in old Frisian and Anglo-Saxon; and a comparison of the every day speech of the country people, presents striking correspondence with various local dialects in England. A system of parallel changes has gone on the two languages.

A BRIEF VIEW OF FRISIAN FORMS AND INFLECTIONS.

VOWELS IN FRISIAN.[1]

In many cases the quantity of the vowel cannot be determined definitely, but may be inferred from a comparison with the other Germanic dialects. Heyne calls attention to the remarkable presentation in Frisian, as in Gothic, of sentences in which the primitive vowels *a, i, u* predominate, as

And thiu pund tha frama, thet skelma ligta oppa en end twintich schillinga.—Emsiger, Kesta, II.

Alsa thi asega nimth tha unriuchta mida and tha urlouada panninga. —Rustringer, Kesta, III.

In other sentences the vowel *e* predominates.

Ief Fresona capmen and thera sogen stretena engere wertha benet.— Emsiger, Kesta, IX.

I § Short Vowels. A.

i. Original *a* is preserved in Frisian before *m* and *n*, either alone or doubled, or joined with mutes, also before a single consonant with *a* or *u* in the following syllable, as *framd*, Ger. *fremd, kanna*, Ger. *kennen, land*, land, *fara*, fare.

ii. The tendency to become *o* is also manifest, as *man* man and *mon, land* and *lond.*

iii. An *e* in the final syllable produces umlaut, as *hangst. hengstes*, Ger. *Hengst.*

iv. With a doubled consonant following, *a* remains generally before combinations with *l* and *x*; before *r* the umlaut appears as *falla*, fall; *waxa*, increase; *berd*, beard.

The earliest Frisian forms in the Lex Frisonum present less frequent cases of umlaut, as *magad*, maid for later *megith.*

---

[1] See *Heyne's Laut und-Flexiouslehre*, 3d ed. Compare *Rask's Friesche Spraakleer.* Translated into Dutch by M. Hettema; also, *Helfenstein's Comparative Grammar of the Teutonic Language.*

E.

i. E appears derived from *a*, *i* and *u*; from *a* in two ways, by umlaut as *henda* (to take) from *hand*, hand, and secondly like the Anglo-Saxon *ä* from *a*, by a simple weakening of the sound   This is especially common in the preterit of strong verbs as *brek* from *breka*, break, *jef* from *ieva*, give; also before doubled mutes and combinations with *r*, as *ekker*, acre, *gers*, grass, *bern*, bairn.

ii. E from i. This corresponds with Old Saxon and O. H. G. *ë* in *helm*, as *hilpa*, held, *swester*, sister.   The vowel *e* is not changed in the conjugation of strong verbs in the present tense. hence, *bersta*, burst, *berstet*.

iii. E appears for original *u*, often through an intermediate change into *o*, *fella*, full.

In the participles *helen*, concealed, *breken*, broken, and in similar verbs the *e* represents the vowel of the infinitive where other verbs have *o*. A.-S. *gebrocen*.

I.

i. I remains unchanged in Frisian in many combinations especially when followed by *m* and *n* as *himul*, Ger. *Himmel*; and before *v* with a dental following, where the A.-S. has *eo*, as *hinder*, hinder; *hirte*, heart, A.-S. *heort*.

ii. I is broken to *iu* before *cht*, as *siucht*, for *siht*, sees; *riucht* for *richt*, right.

O.

i. O represents the obscuring of *u*, as in the other Germanic dialects, *hol*, hole, *boga*, bow. It remains before *m* and *n*, where it often takes the place of *a*, as *nama*, and *noma*, name.

U.

i. U represents an original *u*; it passes into *o*, as *sumur* and *somer*, summer, but holds in general the same position in Frisian as in the other Germanic dialects.

§ 2.   Long Vowels.

A.

i. Long *á* appears in a few words as the representative of the O. H. G. *á*, as *nátha*, O. H. G. *gi-náda*, Mod. Ger. *Gnade*.

ii. Long *á* appears in the auslaut of a few words, as *hwa*, who, A.-S. *hwá*, O. S. *hue*; *twá*, two; *má*, man.

iii. Long *á* appears in a few cases of contraction as *fó*, Ger. *fangen*, Old Eng. *to fang*.

iv. Long *á* appears in Frisian as the representative of the Gothic *au*, A.-S. *ea ;* as *áge*, eye, A.-S. *eáge*, Gothic, *augo ;* *káp*, purchase, Eng. *cheap*, A.-S. *keáp*, G. *kaupon ;* Fr, *gá*, G. *gaujans*, Ger. *Gau*.

v. Long *á* occasionally represents Gothic *ai* as in *ága*, have, G. *aigan ;* *áskia*, ask, A.-S. *áscian*.

vi. Long *á* appears in the preterit plural in the second class of ablaut verbs, as *námon* from *nima*, take.

E.

i. Long *é* represents Gothic *é* as in *mél*, G. *mel*, Ger. *mahl*, A.-S. *mael*.

ii. Long *é* represents the contraction of the diphthong *ei*, G. *ei* or *ai*, *léda*, lead, A.-S. *ledenn*, G. *ga-leiþan ;* *hét*, hot, G. *heito*, O. S. *het*, Mod. Fr. *hiet*.

iii. Long *é* represents the Gothic *au*, A.-S. *ea*, as *néth*, Ger. *Nutzen*, G. *nauþs*, A.-S. *neád*.

iv. Long *é* represents the umlaut of *o*, as *dema*, doom, G. *doms*, A.-S. *dóm*.

v. Long *é* represents the umlaut of *ú* as *héde*, hide, A.-S. *húd*, Lat. *cutis*.

vi. Long *é* occasionally represents the Gothic *iu*, A.-S. *eo ;* *bineta*, rob, O. S. *biniotan*, A.-S. *beneoten*, deprive, G. *ga-niutan*.

vii. Long *é* appears in the root of a few originally reduplicating verbs where *a* appears in the root before combination with *n* as *fá*, *féng*, G. *fahan*, *faifah ;* *i* also appears, as *fíng*

I.

i. Long *í* represents the Gothic *ei*, O. H. G. *í ;* as *mín*, my, G. *meins*.

ii. Long *í* appears in consequence of contraction in a few words, as *nía*, new, G. *niujis*.

iii. Long *í* also appears derived from *ei*, where a gutteral has been vocalized, as *dí* from *deis*, gen, *degis*, day.

O.

i. Long *ó* corresponds to Gothic and A.-S. *ó*, O. H. G. *u*, as F. *bróther*, also *bróer*, G. *broþar*, O. H. G. *bruder*.

ii. It represents *é* in a few words, as Fr. and A.-S. *móna*, moon, G. *mêna*, O. S. *máno*.

iii. It remains in the preterit of some verbs as *nômon*, took, *kômon*, came.

U.

i. Long *û* represents the long *u* of the other German dialects, as *hûs*, house.

ii. It represents the contraction *iu*, as *flûcht* for *fliucht*.

iii. It appears in the auslaut in cases of contraction in monosyllables, as *hûa*, hang, *dûa*, do.

3 §   DIPHTHONGS.

Old Frisian has the single diphthong *iu*, with the variations *io* and *ia*; *io* and *iu* appear in words where *io* or *u* is found in the following syllable, *ia* where an *a* appears in the final syllable. The Rustringer dialect retains the weakening *io*, the remaining dialects the fuller *iu*. *Iu* prevails in the auslaut, as *hiu* this; *thiu*, that. In certain strong verbs *ia* remains in the root of the first pers. sing. and *iu* or *io* in the second and third persons sing., as *kiase*, choose, *kiosest*, *kioseth*, pl. *kiasath*.

EI.

Ei is a later formation, occurring in cases of contraction, especially in the terminations, *ag*, and *eg*, as *wei*, way, gen. *wiges* or *weies*, dat. *wige* or *wei*; so also in *dei*, day, gen. *deges* or *deis*; *kei*, key, A.-S. *caeg*; *brein*, brain, A.-S. *braegan*; *leid* for *legad*, laid. In the plural of nouns the *g* again appears as *dega* or *degar*, days.

ii. Ei frequently become *í*, for *dei*, *dí*.

iii. Ei for *e* corresponds to *ei* in a few forms in O. H. G. and O. S., in place of an original *a*, as *deil*, *del*, dale and dell, O. S. *dal*, O. H. G. *tal*, Norse *dal*.

iv. Ei also appear where other dialects exhibit *u*, *iu* and *ou*, as *breid*, bride, A.-S. *brýd*, O. S. *brûd*, Icelandic, *bruðr*.

v. Ei appears also as a weakening of *ai* in foreign words, *keisar*, *caesar*, A.-S. *casere*, O. S. *kêsur*.

vi. *Au* appears developed from *â* by a *w* following, as *blâ*, *blauw*, blue.

4 § WEST-LAUWERS VOWELS.

I. SHORT VOWELS.

i. The umlaut of the *a* is more uniform.

ii. The tendency of *a* to become *o* is less frequent, hence *man,* man, *hand,* hand.

iii. I is a frequent substitute for other vowels:

i. Before *l, m, n* and *r*, it frequently takes the place of *a;* as in *bird,* beard, where the other dialects have *e,* as *berd,* Ger. and Icl. *bart; schil,* shall; *hinxt* for *hengst; nimmer* for *nammêr.*

ii. Similarly *i* takes the places of *e* before liquids in *birg,* Ger. *berg;* of *u* in *stirta,* East Fr. *sterta,* O. H. G. *sturzen.*

O before *n* with a following consonant usually takes the place of *u,* as *jong* for jung.

BREAKING.

I before *l* is often broken; becoming *ie, ielder,* elder.

LONG VOWELS.

Long *á* appears for the East Frisian *é* in the preterit plural of certain strong verbs, as *ságen,* seen, East Frisian *segin.*

DIPHTHONGS.

1. *Ie* stands for E. Fr. *ia,* as *tziesa* for *kiasa,* choose.
2. *Io* stands occasionally for E. Fr. *iu.*
3. *Au* and *ou* appear later, produced by the dropping of *l,* as *goud* for *gold,* and *saut* for *salt.*

The combinations *hw, kw, sw, dw, tw* and *thw,* remain in the anlaut, where in English the *w* has become vocalized, as in *which,* (*huitsch*).

§ 5. CONSONANTS.

LIQUIDS.

The Liquids *l, m, n, r*, correspond in general to the Anglo-Saxon.

M in endings has become *n.* In the inlaut *n* is dropped, as in the Anglo-Saxon, before *s, f* and *th;* hence *us* for *uns,* us, *fif* for *finf,* five, *muth* for *munth,* mouth, and *-ath* for *-and* in the plural terminations of the present, as *ner-ath* for *ner-and.* In the termination of the infinitive *n* has been dropped. It reappears however in the gerundive, as *werthande.*

The metathesis of *r* is common, as *kersten* for *kristen, gers* for *gres,* grass, *warold* for *wrold,* world, *hars* and *hors* for O. H. G. *hros.*

Rhotacismus is common, *was,* was, pl. *wéron.*

SPIRANTS, *w, f, r, j, th, s, z.*

i. *W.* The Anglo-Saxon tendency to vocalize the *w* only appears in a few cases as in the Brokmer and Emsiger *suster* for the Rustringer *swester*, also in *kuma* for *kvema*, come. ii. *W* in the inlaut corresponds to O. H. G. *w*, as *triuwe, triwa*, true. iii. In the auslaut *w* remains, or is dropped, with the lengthening of the preceding vowel, *frôwe*, Ger. *Frau, trê*, tree, G. *triu*, A.-S. *treow.*

H. CH.

i. In the inlaut, *h* is often dropped, as *tian*, Eng. ten, O. S. *tehan*, or becomes *g*, as from *stâ*, Eng. slay, pret. *slôgon.*

ii. *Ch* stands for *h* in the auslaut, and before *t* in the inlaut, *hâch*, high, *achta*, eight.

J.

J is represented by *i* in the manuscripts.

It represents an original spirant *j*, also *g* in other dialects. It is frequently vocalized when final.

i. In derivatives from *ja* stems and in inflection it is vocalized and does not again appear; *jér*, year, *ieva* and *geva*, give, *hiri*, G. *hirjis*, army, gen. *hiri.*

S.

S corresponds to *s* in O. S. and O. H. G. *sc.* It becomes *sch* in the Emsiger dialect before *e* and *i.* In the preterit plural of many verbs, *r* takes the place of *s*, *kiase*, choose, pret. *kas*, pl. *keron.* *Z* appears in later Frisian.

F. V.

F represents the labial aspirate, *ph* in the anlaut, also in the inlaut before *n* or a dental mute, and in the auslaut.

V appears in the inlaut, *gréf*, grave, gen. *greves.*

The gemination of *f* occurs only in foreign words.

MUTES.

LABIALS.

P initial appears in but few native Frisian words. It remains on the same step as in the Gothic. The labial aspirate *ph* has passed into the spirant *f* or *v.* *B* initial remains unchanged, as also in cases of gemination, and in the combination *mb*, otherwise it passes into the aspirate.

PALATALS.

i. The palatals *g* and *k* are in a few words represented by *j* before and *ie*, as *jild* for geld; *iet* for *gat*, hole, Eng. gate.

ii. *K* in the anlaut may become *sz* or *sth*, *ts*, *tz* or *tsz*. *K* in the inlaut before *t* becomes *ch*, as *séka*, seek, *sôchta*, *mega*, may, *máchta*.

iii. *G* remains generally unchanged in the anlaut. *G* in the inlaut is often vocalized; *gg* in the inlaut may become *dz*, or is vocalized, as A.-S. *leggian*, O. H. G. *legjan*, Fr. *lega* or *lidza*, or *leia*.

LINGUALS.

The lingual mutes correspond in general to the same letters in Anglo-Saxon. *T* final is sometimes dropped after *ch*, as *riuch* for *riucht*; it stands occasionally for the ending -*th* of verbs, as *nima-t* for *nima-th*, takes; otherwise it occupies the same position as in the other Low German dialects.

The lingual aspirate appears only as *th*. It may have had a softer sound in the inlaut and auslaut, like the Anglo-Saxon ð.

In the inlaut *d* is protected from change by a preceding *n*, as *binda*, bind; the combination *nth* drops the *n*; *d* final remains, except in the terminations of verbs, where it becomes *th*, as *werp-th* for *werp-d*.

LETTERS DROPPED.

H and *w* are often dropped when initial and a previous word is joined to the one they begin, as *nella* for *ne wella*.

WEST FRISIAN CONSONANTS.

i. *N* remains before *th*, as in *munth*.

ii. Initial *hl*, *hr*, *hu* and *hw* lose their aspiration and become generally *r*, *l*, *n*, *w*; *thw* becomes *dw*.

iii. *Sk* becomes *sch*. iv. The spirants *f* and *v* in the inlaut and auslaut are frequently dropped, as *sterva*, die, Eng. starve, part. *sturen* and *storn*. This occurs generally after *r*.

DROPPING OF CONSONANTS.

This is especially frequent in the inlaut, and affects principally the dentals, and corresponds to similar disappearance in the Netherlandish, as *broer* for brôther, *moer*, môder.

§ 6. THE FRISIAN VERB.

The verb has two tenses, present and preterit. The future and perfect tenses are formed by the auxiliaries, *skila*, *hebba*, *wesa*; *wertha* is used in forming the passive.

There are four moods, indicative, subjunctive, imperative and infinitive. Verbs are divided into two classes, strong and weak. The absence of complete forms makes it impossible to classify accurately these verbs. The analogy of those which present fuller forms must often be taken, also that of the other dialects to determine the quantity of the vowels, and the class to which each verb belongs.

The following table exhibits the different classes of strong verbs:

REDUPLICATING VERBS.				ABLAUT-VERBS.			
Present.	Pret.	Part.		Pres.	Pret. Sing.	Plur.	Part.
1. a.	î. ê.	a.	1. i, e.	a.	u.	u.
2. ê.	î, ê.	ê.	2. i, e.	a, e.	â, ê.	i, e.
3. ê.	î, ê.	ê.	3. î.	ê.	i.	i.
4. â.	(î, io? ô).	â, ê.	4. iu, ia, (û).	â.	e.	e.
5. ô, ê.	(î, io?).	ô, ê.	5. a, e.	ô.	ô.	a, e.

Traces of previous reduplication have been greatly obscured. Long *é* represents in most dialects the previous reduplication. Long *i* appears in the Rustringer before *n*, but elsewhere *é*, as *fâ*, *fêng*, to seize.

In the first class of ablaut-verbs *i* appears in the present before *n*; doubled or in combination with a mute, *u* is retained in the participle as *winna*, *wan*, *wunnon*, win.

In the second class of ablaut-verbs *i* remains in root, ending in a vowel, *sia*, see, also in verbs formed with the lengthened root in *ja*. The preterit plural has *â* before *m*, as *nima*, *nam* and *nom*, *nômon*, otherwise *e* in the sing. and *é* in the plural. The vowel of the present remains unchanged in inflection in all forms of the present.

STRONG CONJUGATION.

INDICATIVE PRESENT.			SUBJUNCTIVE.	
Sing. 1. finde	kiase		finde,	kias-e.
2. find-e-st, finst	kios-e-st, kiost,		finde,	kias-e.
3. find-e-th, fint,	kios-e-th, kiost,		finde,	kias-e.
Plur. 1. find-a-th,	kias-a-th,		finde,	kias-e.
2. find-a-th,	kaas-a-th,		finde,	kias-e.
3. find-a-th,	kias-a-th,		finde,	kias-e.

PRET.				
Sing. 1. fand,	kâs,		fund-e,	ker-e.
2.			fund-e,	ker-e.
3. fand,	kâs,		fund-e,	ker-e.
1. fund-on,	ker-o-n,		fund-e,	ker-e.
2. fund-on,	ker-o-n,		fund-e,	ker-e.
3. fund-on,	ker-o-n,		fund-e,	ker-e.

Imp.		Participles.	
Sing. 2. find,	kios,	find-and,	kias-a-nd.
Plur. 2. find-a-th,	kias-a-th,	find-en,	ker-en.
Inf. find-a,	kias-a.		

For *e* in the 2d and 3d persons sing, *i* is often found, as *ist, ith.*
The subjunctive drops *n* in the plural of both tenses. When the characteristic connecting vowel in the 2d and 3d persons, sing. is dropped and the personal endings are joined to a dental *d-st* becomes *st;* *th-st* becomes *st;* *d-th* and *s-st* become *t.* The tendency of the ending *th* to become *t* is also manifest. Rhotacism takes place is dissyllabic preterits.

REDUPLICATING VERBS.

Pres.		Pret.		Part.
1.	a,	î, ê,		a.
2.	ê,	î, ê,		ĉ.
3.	ê,	î, ê,		ĉ.
4.	â, (î),	(î, io),		û, ê, (ô).
5.	ô, ê,	(î, io, ô),		ô, ê.

FIRST CLASS.

bonna,) banna,)		bên,	bênnon,	) bonnen.) bannen, w.
fâ,	seize,	fêng,	fêngon,	) efangen.) fenszen.
falla,	fall,	fôl, w.	fôlen, w.	fallen.
gunga,		gêng,	gêngon,	gangen.
hald,	hold,	hîld,	hîldon,	halden.
hûa,	hang,	hêng,	——	) huen.) huinsen.

SECOND CLASS.

blâ,	blow,	blê,		——
lîta,	let,	lît,	——	lêten.
rêda,	advise,	rêd,	——	——
slêpa,	sleep,	——	——	slêpen,

THIRD CLASS.

hêta,	call,	hît,	hîton,	hêten.
swêpa,	sweep,	——	——	——

FOURTH CLASS.

âka,	increase,	——	——	âken.
hawa,	hew,			) hâwen.) hauwen.
hlâpa,	run,	hlêp,	——	hlêpen.
stêta,	push,	——	——	stôten.

FIFTH CLASS.

flôka,	curse,	——	——	eflôkin.
hrôpa,	call,	[rop.]	——	) hrôpen.) hrêpen.
wêpa,	weep,	——	——	wêpen.

ABLAUT VERBS.

	Pres.	Pret. Sing.	Pret. Plur.	Part.
1.	i, e,	a,	u,	u,
2.	i, e,	a, e,	â, ê,	i, e,
3.	î,	ê,	i,	i,
4.	iu, ia, (û),	â,	e,	e,
5.	a, e,	ô,	ô,	a, e.

FIRST CLASS.

bersta,	*burst,*	——	——	bursten.
binda,	*bind,*	band,	banden, w.	bunden.
brîda?	*draw,*	——	——	brûden,
delva,	*delve,*	——	——	dulven.
derva,	*Ger. derben,*	derf. w.		——
drinka,	*drink,*	——	——	drunken.
finda,	*find,*	fand,	funden.	efunden.
gelda, ⎫ ielda, ⎭	*worth,*	gald,	gulden,	gulden.
bi-ginna, ⎫ bi-ienna, ⎭	*begin,*		gonnen, w.	gunnen.
helpa,	*help,*	——	hulpon,	hulpen.
[h] werva,	*turn,*	——	——	——
kerva,	*cut,* (carve),	— —	——	kurven.
kringa,	*acquire,*	——	krungon,	krungen.
renna,	⎰ *flow,* ⎱ *(run),*	ran,	——	runnen.
singa,	*sing,*	sang,	——	——
skelda,	*scold,*	——	——	skouden.
springa,	*spring,*	sprung, w.		——
sterva,	*die,*	——	sturvon,	sturven.
swinga,	*swing,*			
thwinga,	*force,*	thwang,	thwungon,	thwungen.
werpa,	*throw,*	——	wurpon,	wurpen.
willa,	*soil,*			wullen.
winna,	*win,*	wan,	wunnon,	wunnen.

SECOND CLASS.

Pres.		Pret. Sing.	Pret. Plur.	Part.
bera,	*bear,*	——	——	beren.
bidda,	*beg,*	bed,	bîdon,	biden.
breka,	*break,*	brek,	brêkon,	breken.
eta,	*eat,*	——	——	etten.
ita,				
bi-fella,	*command,*	bi-fel, bi-fâl,	bi-fêlen,	bi-felen. bi-fôlen.
fiuchta,	*fight,*	——	fuchton,	fuchten.
ia,	*affirm,*	iech,	——	eien.
ieva,	*give,*	ief,	ievon,	ieven.
kuma,	*come,*	⎰ kom, ⎱ kam,	kômon, ⎱ kâmon, ⎭	ekimin.

lesa,	*read,*	——	——	gelesen.
liga, ⎱ liflsa, ⎰	*lie,*	lai, w.	——	lidsen.
meta,	*measure,*	met,	——	——
nima,	*take,*	nam,	nûmon,	nimen.
sia,	*see,*	sach,	sâgon,	sien,
sitta,	*sit,*	set,	——	seten,
skera,	*shear,*	sker,	——	eskeren,
skia,	*happen,*	ske,	——	esken.
spreka,	*speak,*	sprek,	sprêkon,	spreken.
stela,	*steal,*	——	stêlon,	stelen.
wega,	*move,*	——	——	——

Third Class.

Pres.		Pret. Sing.	Pret. Sing.	Part.
bîta,	*bite,*	——	——	bitin.
blîka,	*glance,*	——	——	bliken.
drîva,	*drive,*	——	——	driven.
glîda,	*glide,*	——	——	gliden.
grîpa,	*grasp,*	grêp,	gripen,	gripen.
(h)lîa,	*confess,*	——	——	hlien.
(h)nîga,	*bow,*	——	hnigun,	——
kivia, ⎱ szîvia, ⎰	*chide,*	——	——	——
krîga ?	*obtain,*	——	——	——
bi-lîva,	*remain,*	bilêf,	——	——
mîda,	*avoid,*	——	——	——
rîda,	*ride,*	——	reden,	riden.
rîva,	*rive,*	——	——	eriven.
skîna,	*shine,*	——	——	——
skrîva,	*write,*	skrêf,	——	eskriven.
snîda,	*cut,*	——	——	snithen.
spîa,	*spit,*	——	——	espien.
stîga,	*ascend,*	——	——	——

Fourth Class.

Pres.		Pret. Sing.	Pret. Plur.	Part.
biada,	*offer,*	bâd,	bedon,	beden.
briuwa,	*brew,*	——	——	browen.
brûka,	*use,*	——	——	bruken.
driaga,	*deceive,*	——	——	drein.
driapa,	*drip,*	——	——	——
flia,	*flee,*	(flâch),	flegon,	flain.
fliaga,	*fly,*	——	——	——
fliata,	*flow,*	flât,	——	——
kiasa,	*choose,*	kâs,	keron,	ekeren.
kriapa,	*creep,*	——	——	——
ur-liasa,	*lose,*	——	——	leren.
lûka,	*lock,*	——	——	⎱ leken. letzen. ⎰

lûka,	*draw,*	——	——	letzen.
skiata,	*shoot,*	——	——	esketen.
sliapa,	*slip,*	——	——	——
slûta,	*shut,*	slât,	——	——
sprûta,	*sprout,*	——	——	——
tia,	*draw,*	tâch,	tegon,	tein.

FIFTH CLASS.

Pres.		Pret. Sing.	Pret. Plur.	Part.
drega,	*drew,*	drôch,	drôgon,	dregen.
fara,	*fare,*	fôr,	fôron,	faren.
heva,	*heave,*	hôf,	hôven,	geheven.
hlada,	*load,*	——	——	hleden.
skeppa,	*make,*	skôp,	skôpon.	skepen.
slâ,	*strike,*	slôch,	slôgon,	{ slain. { slagen.
swera,	*swear,*	swör,	swôren,	sweren.
waxa,	*wax,*	wôx,	wôxon,	waxen.
wada,	*wade,*	wôd,	——	——

Irregular forms are seen in *dua,* do, *dede, deden, edên, dên* and *gedân ; wesa,* be, *wes, wêron, wesen ; stân,* stand, *stôd, stôdon, estenden.*

WEAK CONJUGATION.

Two forms of verbs are preserved as in the Anglo-Saxon and Old Saxon. They correspond in part to the Gothic weak verbs, in *ja* and *ô.* The connecting vowel of the preterit of these verbs is the weakened *e,* as *nera, nerede,* or *nerde.*

In many verbs gemination has taken place, developed by the *ja* of the lengthened root, as *sella,* O. S. *sellian,* A.-S. *sellan,* Icl. *selja ; thekka,* deck, A.-S. *þeccan,* O. H. G. *thecian ; seka,* say, A.-S. *secgan,* O. S. *seggian ;* also in *tella,* tell, O. H. G. *zaljan,* A.-S. *talian.*

The preterit is formed by adding *de* or *te* to the root, verbs ending in a liquid, or sonant mute, or simple *s* which join the termination directly to the root without a connecting vowel, add *de* to form the preterit; verbs ending in a surd mute or double *s* add *te* to form the preterit, as in the Old Saxon. The past participle adds *d* to roots whose vowel is long, *id* or *ed* to roots whose vowel is short. When the preterit is formed by adding *te,* the participle ends in *t ; lêra,* teach, *lêrde, wisa,* point out, *wisde ; thekka,* deck, *thachta ; resta,* rest, pret. *reste.* What is termed for convenience *rückumlaut* appears in a few verbs, ending in *k,* as *sêka,* seek, *sôchte,* G. *sokjan.*

The termination of the O. S. preterit, -da, connecting vowels *i* and *o*, Anglo-Saxon *de*, connecting vowels *e* and *ó*, is in Frisian *de*, with the connecting vowels *e* and *a* ; compare O. S. *ner-i-da*, and *seaw-ó-da* ; A.-S. *ner-e-de*, and *sealf-ó-de* ; Frisian *ner-e-de*, and *sealf-a-de*. The forms which still show a *j* in the present tense are often further lengthened to *-ige-*, *-ege-*, *-igi-*, as *endia*, end, *endigia*, *endgia*.

FIRST WEAK CONJUGATION.

INDICATIVE MOOD.

Present Tense.	First Weak Conjugation.	Second Weak Conjugation.
Sing. 1. ner-e,	sêk-e,	âsk-je.
2. ner-i-st, ner-st,	sêk-i-st, sêk-st,	âsk-a-st.
3. ner-ith, ner-th,	sêk-i-th, sêk-th,	âsk-a-th.
1. ner-a-th,	sêk-a-th,	âsk-ja-th.
2. ner-a-th,	sêk-â-th,	âsk-ja-th.
3. ner-a-th,	sêk-a-th,	âsk-ja-th.
Preterit.	*Preterit.*	*Preterit.*
Sing. 1. ner-e-de, nerde,	sôch-te,	âsk-a-de.
2. ner-e-dest,	sôch-test,	âsk-a-dest.
3. ner-e-de,	sôch-te,	ûsk-a de.
Plur. 1. ner-e-don, ner-don,	sôch-ton,	âsk-a-don.
2. ner-e-don,	sôch-ton,	âsk-a-don.
3. ner-e-don,	sôch-ton,	âsk-a-don.

SUBJUNCTIVE MOOD.

Present.	Present.	Present.
Sing. 1. ner-i (e)	sêk-i (e)	âsk-je.
2. ner-i,	sêk-i,	âsk-je.
3. ner-i,	sêk-i,	âsk-je.
Plur. 1. ner-i,	sêk-i (e)	âsk-je.
2. ner-i,	sêk-i,	âsk-je.
3. ner-i,	sêk-i,	âsk-je.
Preterit.		
Sing. 1. ner-de,	sôch-te,	âsk-a-de.
2. ner-de,	sôch-te,	âsk-a-de.
3. ner-de,	sôch-te,	âsk-a-de.
Plur. 1. ner-de,	sôch-te,	âsk-a-de.
2. ner-de,	sôch-te,	âsk-a-de.
3. ner-de,	sôch-te,	âsk-a-de.
Imperative.		
Sing. 2. ner-e,	sêke,	âsk-ja.
Plur. 2. nerath,	sek-ath,	âsk-ja-th.
Inf. nera,	sêka,	âsk-ja.
Part. nerand,	sek-and,	âsk-ja-nd.
nerid,	sôch-t,	âsk-a-d.

ANOMALOUS VERBS.

Impf.		Pres. Sing.	Pres. Plural.	Pret.
I. kunna,	*know,*	kan,	konnen, konath.	konde.
thura,	*dare,*	thur,	thuron,	thorste.
thurva,	{ *need,* { *be allowed,*	thurf,	thurvon.	
II. skila,	*owe,*	skil,	skiln,	skolde.
mega,	*able,*	mei, mî,		machte.
III. âga, }				
hâga, }	*have,*	âch,	âgon,	âchte.
wita,	*know,*	wêt, wit,		
IV. duga,	*to be worth,*	duch,		
V. môta?	*must,*	môt,		môste.

WEST-LAUWERS VERBS.

The distinguishing features of these verbs are in brief:

1. The changes by ablaut are not uniform in verbs of the first class, as *binda, band, banden, bonden ; helpa, hulp, hulpen, hulpen.*

2. The tendency to employ *o* instead of *u* in the preterit and participle.

3. The fourth ablaut-class shows *ie* for *ia, io* for *iu.*

4. The fuller vowels in the endings of inflection have become *e.*

5. The *th* of the third person singular and the plural is *t* or *d.*

6. A few infinitives, and the subjunctive in the plural show *n,* as *gân,* go, *quân,* say.

§ 7. DECLENSION OF NOUNS.

STRONG DECLENSION.

A-DECLENSION.

		Masculine.	Feminine.	Neuter.	
Sing.	Nom.	fisk,	jeve,	word,	skip,
	Gen.	fiski-s, (-es),	jeve,	word-is, -es,	skipi-s, -es.
	Dat.	fisk-a, -e, -i,	jebe,	word-a, -e,	skipa, -e.
	Acc.	fisk,	jeve,	word,	skip.
Plur.	Nom.	fiskar, -a,	jeva,	word (a),	skipu, -o.
	Gen.	fisk-a,	jeve-n-a,	word-a,	skip-a
	Dat.	fisk-um, -on, -em,	jevu-m, -on,	wordu-m, -on,	skipu-m, -on.
	Acc.	fiska, -ar,	jeva,	word-a,	skipu, -o.

The masculine nominative plural exhibits two forms in *-a* and *-ar.* When *r* is omitted the plural corresponds to that of the weak declension. Compare O. H. G. neuters in *-ir* and Icl. masculine and neuters in *-ar.*

The genitive singular of the masculine and neuter nouns in *is*, is retained in the Rustringer dialect, while the other dialects exhibit the weakened *es*.

The dative in *a* is retained in the Hunsingoer and Emsiger dialects. The Rustringer has *i* and the Brokmer *e*.

In the dative plural the Rustringer has *on*, the Brockmer *um* and the other dialects *em*. When in the feminine singular *a* appears in the oblique cases, the forms of the strong and weak declensions correspond. The genitive plural has often *a* instead of *ena*, O. H. G. *ônô*, A.-S. *ena*. Neuter nouns have in the plural two forms according as the root has a long or short vowel. The short syllabled neuters show *u* as in the A.-S. and O. S., commonly represented by *o*, Emsiger *e ;* the long-syllabled show *a* as *jêr*, year, pl. *jéra*. Dissyllabic neuters in *el* and *en* form the plural in *e*, weakened from *u*, as in the Anglo-Saxon, as *bêken*, beacon, pl. *bêkene*. Compare A.-S. *beácen,*pl. *beácenu.*

Of themes in *ja* no traces are left, except in the termination *-e* of the nom. sing. of a few masc. and neut. nouns, as *hôdere*, hat-bearer. *I* appears for *j-* vocalized in *hiri*, army, G. *harjis*.

I-DECLENSION.

This declension contains only masculine and feminine nouns. Only four masculine nouns remain, *liode*, Ger. *Leute*, only found in the plural; *fôt*, foot, pl. *fêt ; toth*, tooth, both of which belonged to the *u*-declension originally. The feminine nouns are declined like nouns of the same class in Anglo-Saxon. The dative plural shows the forms *-im, -em, -um, -on.*

Masculine, *fôt*, foot.   Feminine, *nêd*, need.

Sing. N. fôt,	nêd,
G. fôte-s,	nêde.
D. fôte,	nêde.
A. fôt,	nêde.
Plur. N. fêt,	nêda, -e.
G. fôt-a,	nêda.
D. fôte-m, -on,	nêd-im, -em, -um, -on.
A. fêt,	nêda.

U-DECLENSION.

This declension retains but two masculine nouns *sunu*, son, *fretho*, peace, and the neuter *fia*, Ger. *vieh*, G. *failhu*.

Masculine, Sing. N. sunu, -o, G. suna, D. suna, A. sunu.
     Plur. N. sun-ar, -a, G. (suna), D. sun-um, A. sun-a-r, -a.
Neut. N. fia, G. fias, D. and A. fia.

WEAK DECLENSION.

	Masculine.	Feminine.		Neuter.
Sing. N.	hona, cock,	tunge, tongue,	âge, eye,	âre, ear.
G.	hona,	tunga,	âga,	âra.
D.	hona,	tunga,	âga,	ara.
A.	hona,	tunge,	age,	âre.
Plur. N.	hona,	tunga,	âgon.	âra.
G.	honan-a, (-ona),	tungan-a,	agen-a? agen,	ûren-a.
D.	honu-m,	tungum,	agenu-m,	âru-m.
A.	hona,	tunga,	âgon, âgene,	âra.

The Emsiger, Hunsingoer and Fivelgoer dialects exhibit a tendency to restore the *u* which has been lost, as *frôwe*, Ger. Frau, *frôwan*.

CONSONANT STEMS IN -*R* AND -*AND*.

Sing. N.	brôther,		friund, friond.
G.	brôther-es (-s),		friunde-s.
D.	brôther-e,		friunde.
A.	brôther,		friund.
Plur. N.	brôther-a (-e),		friund.
G.	brôther-a (-e),		friund-a.
D.	brôther-um,		friund-um, -on, -em.
A.	brôther-a, -e,		friund.

The feminine nouns *môder*, mother, *swester*, sister, and *dochter*, daughter, are declined in the same way. The genitive singular may have -*e* instead of -*s*, as *môdere*.

§ 8. DECLENSION OF ADJECTIVES.

STRONG DECLENSION.

	Masculine.	Feminine.	Neuter.
Sing. N.	blind,	blind-e,	blind.
G.	blind-es,	blind-ere, (-re),	blind-es.
D.	blind-a, (-e),	blind-ere, (-re),	blind-a, (-e).
A.	blind-ene, (-ne, -en),	blind-e,	blind.
Plur. N.	blind-a, (-e),	blind-a, (-e),	blind-a, (-e).
G.	blind-era, (-ra),	blind-era, (-ra),	blind-era, (-ra).
D.	blind-a, (-e),	blind-a, (-e),	blind-a, (-e).
A.	blind-a, (-e),	blind-a, (-e),	blind-a, (-e).

WEAK DECLENSION.

	Masculine.	Feminine.	Neuter.
Sing. N.	blind-a,	blind-e,	blind-e.
G.	blind-a,	blind-a,	blind-a.
D.	blind-a,	blind-a,	blind-a.
A.	blind-a,	blind-a,	blind-e.
Plur. D.	blind-a,	blind-a,	blind-a.
G.	blind-ena,	blind-ena,	blind-ena.
D.	blind-um,	blind-um,	blind-um.
A.	blind-a,	blind-a,	blind-a.

Participles both present and perfect are declined like adjectives of the strong and weak declension The present participle when uninflected shows a final *e* from a fuller formative *j*, as *findande*.

The infinitive has a dative form in *e*, before which it resumes the consonant *n*, lost from the infinitive as *to farane*, to fare. The Rustringer dialect shows the form *to farande*, as if influenced by the present participle.

Adjectives are compared by means of the suffixes *ir* and *or*, and *ist*, *ost* and *ast*. The weakened forms *er* and *est* are frequent. The old comparison in *m* is preserved in *for-m-a* first, superlative *for-m-est*. Adjectives in the comparative degree are inflected only according to the weak declension, those in the superlative degree, according to both the strong and weak declensions.

The numerals afford no especial occasion for remark. They present few variations from Anglo-Saxon and Old Saxon forms.

WEST LAUWERS DECLENSION.

This dialect shows a tendency to form the plural of masculine nouns from vowel themes in *n*. as *êth*, oath, plural, *êthan*. The feminine nouns do not exhibit this tendency in the same degree.

§ 9. PRONOUNS.

PERSONAL PRONOUNS.

	1 Pers.	II Pers.	III.	III Pers. Mas.	III Pers. Fem.	III Pers. Neut.
Sing. N.	ik,	thu,		hi, he.	hiu, sê,	hit.
G.	mîn,	thîn,	sîn,	[sîn],	hiri,	[sîn].
D.	mi,	thi,		him,	hiri,	him.
A.	mi,	thi,		hini, (-e, -a),	hia, sê,	hit.
Plur. N.	wi,	i, gi,			hia, sê.	
G.	úser,	iuwer,			hira, hiara.	
D.	ús,	iu, io,			him, hiam,	
A.	ús,	iu, io,			hia, sĉ.	

For the pronoun of the third person, is used the demonstrative *hi* as in Anglo-Saxon, and in the nominative masculine of the Old Saxon. The genitive singular, masculine and neuter, is supplied by the form *sin*, not marking gender, as in O. H. G. There is a marked tendency to join the nominative of this pronoun, to other forms of the same pronoun and to the demonstrative, as *hit* for *hi hit; hint* for *hin hit; hitha* for *hit tha.*

The indefinite *ma*, Ger. man, is early distinguished from the concrete *man* or *mon*. It is often joined to a following pronoun, as *mas*, for *ma thes.*

POSSESSIVE ADJECTIVE PRONOUNS.

mîn *and* mein,	*my.*	unser *and* W. F. ouse,	*our.*
thîn *and* dein,	*thy.*	iuwe, " iuwer,	*your.*
sîn,	*his, its.*		

The inflection is like that of the strong adjective. The effort to form a possessive from the feminine pronoun is early manifest, as *hire kindis* and *hires birnes*, of her child. Compare the similar development of the form *ir*, in Middle High German.

DEMONSTRATIVE PRONOUNS.

		Mas.	Fem.	Neut.
Sing.	Nom.	thi,	thiu,	thet.
	Gen.	thes,	there,	thes.
	Dat.	tham, tha,	there,	tham.
	Acc.	them,	tha,	thet.
	Inst.			thiu.

Plur.	Nom.	tha.
	Gen.	thera.
	Dat.	thâm, thâ.
	Acc.	tha.

The lengthened demonstative from the old forms *tja* and *sa*, is *thi-s.*

		Masculine.	Feminine.	Neuter.
Sing.	Nom.	thi-s, the-s,	thiu-s,	thi-t.
	Gen.	thisses,	thisse,	thisses.
	Dat.	thissa,	thisse,	thissa.
	Acc.	(this-ne),	thisse,	thit.
Plur.	Nom.	thisse, thesse,	thisse,	thisse.
	Gen.	thessera,	thessera,	thessera.
	Dat.	thisse, thesse,	thisse,	thisse.
	Acc.	thisse,	thisse,	thisse.

The demonstrative *jen*, G. *jains*, is wanting in Frisian as in Old Saxon.

INTERROGATIVE PRONOUNS.

		Masculine and Fem.	Neuter.
Sing.	Nom.	hwa,	hwet.
	Gen.	hwammes,	hwammes.
	Dat.	hwam,	hwam.
	Acc.	hwane, hwene,	hwet.

RELATIVE PRONOUNS.

The Frisian uses the demonstrative or the particle *ther* for the relative.

THE INDEFINITE PRONOUNS

Are *Sum*, some, *ek*, each, *monich*, many, *enich*, any, *annen*, one, *nên* and *nanen*, no, one, *ammon*, *immen*, O. S. *eoman*, any one, *awet*, ought, *nawet*, naught, *al*, frequently uninflected, all, *ek*, each.

www.ingramcontent.com/pod-product-compliance
Lightning Source LLC
Chambersburg PA
CBHW031748090426
42739CB00008B/926